Expanding Opportunities for Professional Education

#37

Leila V. Moore, *Editor*
Pennsylvania State University
Robert B. Young, *Editor*
Kent State University

NEW DIRECTIONS FOR STUDENT SERVICES

MARGARET J. BARR, *Editor-in-Chief*
Texas Christian University

M. LEE UPCRAFT, *Associate Editor*
Pennsylvania State University

Number 37, Spring 1987

Paperback sourcebooks in
The Jossey-Bass Higher Education Series

Jossey-Bass Inc., Publishers
San Francisco • London

Leila V. Moore, Robert B. Young (eds.).
Expanding Opportunities for Professional Education.
New Directions for Student Services, no. 37.
San Francisco: Jossey-Bass, 1987.

New Directions for Student Services
Margaret J. Barr, *Editor-in-Chief;* M. Lee Upcraft, *Associate Editor*

New Directions for Student Services is published quarterly
by Jossey-Bass Inc., Publishers (publication number USPS
494-090). Second-class postage paid at San Francisco, California, and at
additional mailing offices. POSTMASTER: Send address changes to
Jossey-Bass Inc., Publishers, 433 California Street, San Francisco,
California 94104.

Editorial correspondence should be sent to the Editor-in-Chief,
Margaret J. Barr, Sadler Hall, Texas Christian University,
Fort Worth, Texas 76129.

Library of Congress Catalog Card Number LC 85-644751

International Standard Serial Number ISSN 0164-7970

International Standard Book Number ISBN 1-55542-970-X

Cover art by WILLI BAUM

Manufactured in the United States of America

Ordering Information

The paperback sourcebooks listed below are published quarterly and can be ordered either by subscription or single copy.

Subscriptions cost $48.00 per year for institutions, agencies, and libraries. Individuals can subscribe at the special rate of $36.00 per year *if payment is by personal check.* (Note that the full rate of $48.00 applies if payment is by institutional check, even if the subscription is designated for an individual.) Standing orders are accepted.

Single copies are available at $11.95 when payment accompanies order. (California, New Jersey, New York, and Washington, D.C., residents please include appropriate sales tax.) For billed orders, cost per copy is $11.95 plus postage and handling.

Substantial discounts are offered to organizations and individuals wishing to purchase bulk quantities of Jossey-Bass sourcebooks. Please inquire.

Please note that these prices are for the academic year 1986–1987 and are subject to change without notice. Also, some titles may be out of print and therefore not available for sale.

To ensure correct and prompt delivery, all orders must give either the *name of an individual* or an *official purchase order number.* Please submit your order as follows:

Subscriptions: specify series and year subscription is to begin.
Single Copies: specify sourcebook code (such as, SS1) and first two words of title.

Mail orders for United States and Possessions, Latin America, Canada, Japan, Australia, and New Zealand to:
Jossey-Bass Inc., Publishers
433 California Street
San Francisco, California 94104

Mail orders for all other parts of the world to:
Jossey-Bass Limited
28 Banner Street
London EC1Y 8QE

New Directions for Student Services Series
Margaret J. Barr, *Editor-in-Chief;* M. Lee Upcraft, *Associate Editor*

Contents

Editors' Notes

Expanding Professional Education for Student Affairs Staff

It was a sign of the times. In its Winter 1984 issue, *College Student Personnel Abstracts* designated "burnout" as a special topic in the literature of the field. Burnout, the occupational illness of the 1980s, and one outcome of the ever-present stress and ever-increasing problems of student affairs staff, has been the topic of innumerable articles, convention programs, staff consultations, and informal conversations during this decade. Burnout, as used here, is defined as "a significant loss of motivation, enthusiasm, and energy . . . [and] a marked departure of the individual from previous normal work and nonwork patterns" (Wiggers, Forney, and Wallace-Schutzman, 1982, p. 12).

Professional burnout is related to educational fatigue. Some practitioners have not maintained their knowledge about the general evolution of the field, about new practices, or about the whys and wherefores of particular problems, such as student mental health, reduced resources, fluctuating enrollments, and special student needs. They feel overwhelmed by the need to know more about their field. They look back at their graduate programs and recognize gaps in their knowledge that have been created by the passing of time or by the emergence of new issues in higher education. Many turn to professional education activities in order to bridge these gaps.

Professional education is a way to revitalize staff members who grow more frustrated as the opportunities for upward or lateral job mobility shrink. To these "stuck" staff members, professional education activities may be a chance to retool their skills or reassess their careers.

For others, the emergence of the *CAS Standards and Guidelines for Student Services/Development Programs* (Council for the Advancement of Standards, 1986) has signaled the need for more education. Used as a guideline for self-study in the accreditation process, the standards refer specifically to the need for professional staff members to have graduate degrees in relevant fields. In addition, they recommend that student affairs programs provide opportunities for continued professional growth of staff members.

In spite of an apparent need for focused attention on professional education, a review of the literature reveals the disorganization of current professional education activities in student affairs. Systematization is lacking. Practitioners tend to modify and add new activities to the staff development repertory, but they seldom consider the reasons behind, direction to, and orchestration of those activities. Student affairs lacks a systematic model that relates the stages of growth of its practitioners to different needs for and modes of professional education.

Our random approach deters our understanding about the impact of these learning activities on developmental needs. Burnout evokes concern about professional revitalization, which in turn raises questions about the contexts, contents, contributors, and constituencies of professional education. What are the developmental needs of practitioners? What needs can be met through graduate education and continuing professional education? Are there relationships between the developmental needs of practitioners and their preferred means of obtaining more education? Who supplies professional education? Who should apply it? How does continuing professional education relate to graduate education? What emerging requirements for new or updated knowledge or skills shape the need for professional education into a demand? Do the career paths of student personnel practitioners influence patterns of professional education? What future research is needed to strengthen professional education activities? Have the developmental needs of any groups of practitioners been neglected in the current conceptions and means of delivering professional education? What are the roles of student affairs staff members, individuals, institutions, and professional organizations in overseeing this important activity?

The questions weave themselves together. They form a tapestry of concern about the vitality of the entire field of student affairs, as well as about the forms of professional education within it. Answers to these questions might benefit individuals and the profession. The purposes of this sourcebook are to provide an update on the state of the student affairs profession, to present a model of professional education, and to review ways in which professional education should be implemented.

The importance of the latter purpose is reflected in the description of a profession, because one of the hallmarks of a profession is its focus on professional education: the introduction and updating of the theory, skills, and perspective of practitioners in the field (Hesburgh, Miller, and Wharton, 1973; Houle, 1980). Other attributes of a profession are important, too—for example, developing standards for admission to the field (Wrenn and Darley, 1949)—but educational activities might be the most important characteristic of a profession. Professional education makes an occupation creative, rather than stagnant; it develops professional status through the improved effectiveness of the persons in that field.

As we reviewed the literature of student affairs, we found new discussions about professional education. Many authors uphold the need to stay up to date, but they seldom pay attention to the evolution of this need in individual careers or in the student personnel field. Certain educational forces affect individuals as well as the student personnel field, and an individual need for new knowledge is related to a general demand for competent practitioners of student affairs.

In this sourcebook, Robert D. Brown (Chapter One) introduces the topic of professional education by assessing the state of the professions and the professionals in it. He presents information about typical career paths of student affairs professionals and suggests the need for a model of professional education. In Chapter Two, Robert B. Young presents just such a model, which integrates stages of professional development with modes of education and types of interpersonal relationships in the field. This model introduces and organizes dimensions of education and development that are explored in detail in subsequent chapters.

In Chapter Three, Leila V. Moore uses the professional education model to diagnose the professional education levels of student affairs practitioners and prescribe appropriate learning activities. Next, she describes professional education programs that might benefit student personnel staff on particular campuses. Finally, through the use of case-study examples, Moore discusses the design of a professional education program that responds both to institutional and to individual staff needs.

In Chapter Four, J. Roger Penn and Jo Anne J. Trow discuss the responsibilities of graduate programs for continuing the education of student affairs practitioners. They describe the need for new teaching methods to accommodate graduate and in-service educational concerns. Their chapter ends with recommendations for the involvement of graduate faculty in expanded professional education.

In Chapter Five, Thomas D. Aceto, William A. Bryan, and Robert B. Young describe three ways through which institutions can expand professional education for student affairs practitioners: in-service programs, professional exchanges of staff, and the development of regional education centers.

In Chapter Six, Marian Schrank and Robert B. Young describe the role of state, regional, and national associations in the professional education of student affairs practitioners. The final chapter of this sourcebook includes a summary of the preceding chapters, as well as some thoughts about a national effort to upgrade and diversify professional education activities for student affairs practitioners. Suggestions for further reading are presented in an annotated bibliography.

This sourcebook moves from concepts to practices, but the direction is less important than the discussion of both. The model in Chapter Two grows out of the need for a dynamic conception of student affairs as a profession. It's meaning lies in its utility as a diagnostic and prescriptive tool.

This sourcebook also moves from broad characteristics of student affairs practice to applications for individual practitioners. Again, the direction is less meaningful than the inclusion of each aspect of professional education. The whole of the profession is fulfilled through the summative development of its practitioners.

Finally, this sourcebook mingles discussion of professional development issues with discussion of educational activities. Issues have not been segregated from programming, nor has educational programming been divided into preservice and in-service activities. Student affairs workers are synergists, people who attend to the development of students through educational programs in their offices and institutions. Concerns and programs are inseparable. The approach to this sourcebook is similar, but the focus is inward, toward the development of ourselves instead of the development of our students. The student affairs "physicians" are asked to engage in self-healing, with subsequent benefits to the "patients" and to the profession.

Leila V. Moore
Robert B. Young
Editors

References

Council for the Advancement of Standards. *CAS Standards and Guidelines for Student Services/Development Programs.* Council for the Advancement of Standards for Student Services/Development Programs, 1986.

Hesburgh, T. M., Miller, P. A., and Wharton, C. R., Jr. *Patterns for Lifelong Learning.* San Francisco: Jossey-Bass, 1973.

Houle, C. O. *Continuing Learning in the Professions.* San Francisco: Jossey-Bass, 1980.

Wiggers, T. T., Forney, D. S., and Wallace-Schutzman, F. "Burnout Is Not Necessary: Prevention and Recovery." *National Association of Student Personnel Administrators Journal,* 1982, *20* (2), 13–21.

Wrenn, G. C., and Darley, J. G. "An Appraisal of the Professional Status of Student Personnel Work. Parts I and II." In E. G. Williamson (ed.), *Trends in Student Personnel Work.* Minneapolis: University of Minnesota Press, 1949.

Leila V. Moore is currently director of Career Path Associates and assistant director for student organizations and program development at the Pennsylvania State University. She was formerly a professor of counseling and student personnel at the State University of New York, Albany, at the Pennsylvania State University, and at Bowling Green State University.

Robert B. Young is associate professor and program adviser for higher education administration and coordinator of faculty development for the College of Education at Kent State University.

*Research provides a snapshot of professional pathways and
suggests professional education needs, but more developmental
and longitudinal research should provide richer insights.*

Professional Pathways and Professional Education

Robert D. Brown

Can you imagine a day in the future when a second-grader will say to his
or her parents, "I want to be a student affairs professional when I grow
up"? Or can you imagine a high school freshman or senior saying to a
counselor, "Where can I find out more information about how you
become a dean of students"? Students do not grow up with aspirations to
pursue student affairs careers. It is also unlikely that you are going to find
many college sophomores or juniors giving serious thought to entering
student affairs positions. It is doubtful that they see student affairs as a
career option for anyone, much less for themselves.

People enter student affairs careers by accident or by quirk, rather
than by design. Undergraduate student assistants in residence halls become
aware that their bosses, residence hall directors, make a living working in
the residence halls. Usually, student assistants enjoy working with students, and staff development training programs provide them with a sense
of belonging to a profession. The student assistants find out that the purpose for their existence is more than maintaining order or replacing light
bulbs. Their mission includes helping students with problems, helping
the floor government get organized, and ensuring that the residents are
aware of other services and options available to them. Some start to ask
themselves, "Could I do this for a living?"

L. V. Moore, R. B. Young (eds.). *Expanding Opportunities for Professional Education.*
New Directions for Student Services, no. 37. San Francisco: Jossey-Bass, Spring 1987.

Another major path of entry for undergraduates is student leadership. Student leaders, involved with planning and implementing campus activities, enjoy the challenge of working with and coordinating student organizations. They discover that the consultants for their organizations are filling service roles by working with different campus organizations and campus activities. Training programs for leadership skills and workshops on student development blend well with their natural interest in working with students in leadership roles. "Why couldn't I do this for several more years?" they wonder.

The career pattern illustrated for residence hall and campus activities staff probably applies nearly as well to positions in other student affairs offices on campus—counseling, financial aid, admissions, or the dean's office. The choice comes rather late in the individual's college years. Student affairs becomes a career option because a practicing student affairs professional served as a role model, and because the student was exposed to the career possibility through a leadership or paraprofessional role activity.

This career-choice pattern has several unique characteristics, although they are not rare. First, student affairs is not a career that an individual can be expected to consider early in life or, indeed, even early in the college years. Second, exposure to the career possibility comes through a role model or mentor. Although this may not be a unique factor compared to exposure to other careers (for example, knowing a doctor, a lawyer, or a merchant), there are several unique qualities to it. Usually it is the student's first exposure to the professional role, and perhaps it is even the student's first awareness that the career possibility exists. The student is probably unaware for some time that the work of his or her role model is even part of a profession. Third, the student has had an opportunity to try out the role as a paraprofessional—as a student assistant, a campus leader, or a work-study employee. Fourth, the student's academic major is, for the most part, irrelevant to the career. A student majoring in biology, history, English, sociology, or psychology may be equally prepared to consider a student affairs career. Fifth, information about career possibilities comes from the model or mentor, and few other people, even other students, know much about what student affairs professionals do. Telling your parents that you are going to graduate school so that you can obtain a job that involves coordinating campus activities or being a housing director probably does not convey the image of a long-lasting career; many parents would not know what it means.

This description is based on my associations with many graduate students, as they have begun their professional training, and on the general literature. The initial career choice and its unique characteristics need to be kept in mind when we examine the career paths of student affairs professionals and explore the implications for their professional education needs. This chapter looks at illustrative research findings, suggests some typical profiles or career scenarios, and suggests several implications.

Research on Career Paths of Student Affairs Professionals

This literature summary on career paths will be illustrative, rather than comprehensive, for several reasons. A comprehensive and analytical summary of the literature could give an unwarranted aura of worth to the research. There are several fine studies of career paths, but examination of nearly one hundred related articles leads me to conclude that the body of knowledge on career paths is woefully inadequate, and that much of the research has been poorly done. Most research reports are cross-sectional studies based on return rates averaging between 40 and 50 percent. It is difficult to find studies that pursue the same samples of professionals over time. Comparisons are made across time to earlier studies, but these usually involve data from different sampling procedures and from different questionnaires. Rarely are the studies based on theoretical premises, although this seems to be a more recent trend (see Carpenter and Miller, 1981; Wood, Winston, and Polkosnik, 1985).

Few studies employ any methodology other than a questionnaire; and, for the most part, the questions focus narrowly on what people were doing last year, what they are doing now, and what they plan to do in the future. Occasionally the researcher has asked, "Why?" Nevertheless, there seldom are probing interviews or searches for relationships among key personal and career-path variables.

This is not to say that the research published thus far is not without value. It provides gross indicators of general career patterns and some basis for speculating about professional education needs; but solid evidence based on theory is lacking. We will have to wait for more theoretically premised, longitudinal studies for a fuller understanding of career decisions and paths in student affairs. Let us look at what the currently available literature has to say.

Three questions form the framework for this examination of the literature: Who gets to the top? Who stays and who leaves the profession? What is the career status of women and minorities?

Who Gets to the Top?

The top of the career-path ladder has been operationally defined, or at least labeled, as the chief student affairs officer at an institution. Most career-path literature focuses on this highest-ranked person. (For examples of other areas, see the summary by Gross, 1978.) Numerous studies have examined characteristics of the chief student affairs officer and looked at turnover patterns.

A profile of chief student affairs officers a decade ago suggested that the overwhelming majority were men (98.1 percent) and Anglos (96 percent); the majority had doctorates (64 percent), and about half (57 percent) had published something (Brooks and Avila, 1974). Their average

8

age was about forty, they had been in their positions slightly under five years, and they had been at their current institutions nearly eight years.

More recent research (Harder, 1983), notes several significant changes in these traditional characteristics. These changes suggest patterns that have implications for the future. Harder's study was based on a regional sample, which may mean that some differences were due to geography, but her findings still merit careful consideration. Among the noteworthy findings were differences in level of educational preparation, type of educational preparation, age and years of experience, and common professional experiences. Of the respondents, 64 percent had the doctorate, compared to 35 percent to 47 percent in earlier studies (Gross, 1978). The larger the institution, the more likely the possession of a terminal degree. Harder (1983) found that 94 percent of the respondents from four-year public institutions possessed doctorates, while Paul and Hoover (1980) reported 83 percent from similar institutions as having the terminal degree.

In the past, the chief student affairs officer did not have training in higher education administration, and there has not been significant change in this pattern. Studies of the past decade or longer indicate that between 27 percent and 48 percent of the chief student affairs officers had degrees in counseling or student personnel, compared to between 7 percent and 24 percent for higher education (Brooks and Avila, 1974; Grant and Foy, 1972; Harder, 1983; Hoyt and Tripp, 1967; Ostroth, Efird, and Lerman, 1984; Paul and Hoover, 1980).

Career-pattern information suggests that common past career experiences include public school teaching (Grant and Foy, 1972). This undoubtedly suggests that student affairs is more a career chosen after several years of college than a conscious step on the career ladder. More pertinent career-path information indicates that chief student affairs officers have often either had general student services administrative experience (dean, assistant dean) or held administrative positions in student services areas, such as housing, counseling, or placement (Harder, 1983; Lunsford, 1984).

One study (Ostroth, Efird, and Lerman, 1984) reported that nearly a third started their student affairs careers in executive positions, although the average administrator was in the profession at least six years before becoming the chief student affairs person. Over half did not intend to become chief officers and had some experience teaching. The average age in this study was forty-four.

The expertise, such as management skills, that student affairs officers find most essential to their work is most often gained through experience, rather than through formal education (Lunsford, 1984). Administrators reported that broad experience was the primary ingredient of their success. Many made the decision to move out of student affairs when it looked as if they would not move up (Lunsford, 1984).

Who Stays and Who Leaves the Profession?

Surveys of master's program graduates seven to ten years after graduation indicate that about 60 percent are still employed in student affairs (Burns, 1982; Holmes, Verrier, and Chisholm, 1983). This is an average rate, however, and by the sixth year after graduation, the original high of 90 percent still in the profession has dropped to 40 percent. These studies, compared to earlier studies, may show greater stability in recent years among stayers. In 1969, 29 percent of a surveyed group had been in the profession eleven years or more, but by 1980 this figure had jumped to 55 percent employed more than eleven years (Grant and Foy, 1972; Holmes, Verrier, and Chisholm, 1983; Lawing, Moore, and Groseth, 1982).

Women are more likely to think about leaving or to be among the leavers than are men (Bender, 1980; Burns, 1982; Holmes, Verrier, and Chisholm, 1983). Single women are more likely to stay than are married women, but married men are more likely to stay than are single men (Bender, 1980; Lawing, Moore, and Groseth, 1982; Moore and Burns, 1983).

Leavers and stayers differ in several ways. Leavers may be less altruistic and more concerned about advancement. In one study (Burns, 1982), leavers placed less importance on dedication, independence, and service and more on leadership, advancement, and expertise than did stayers. Leavers were bored, wanted to relocate geographically, wanted to return to school, and hoped to advance and make more money. Stayers were more likely to have less interrupted careers, and significantly more stayers (83 percent) had their first jobs in student affairs than did leavers (50 percent). Correlates of staying in student affairs include job satisfaction, number of years in student affairs, number of positions, happiness with work, work experience in student affairs prior to a degree, being in a smaller institution, and being published (Lawing, Moore, and Groseth, 1982). It should also be noted that these variables account for only about 30 percent of the total variance. Thus, many other factors affect staying or leaving. For example, mentoring appears to be related to staying in the profession. Stayers were more likely to have mentors than leavers (Holmes, Verrier, and Chisholm, 1983). One must be careful, however, in interpreting this kind of finding. It is difficult to sort out whether other variables were related to the mentoring. Was a self-selection element operating?

When general morale or job satisfaction studies are examined, it is difficult to obtain satisfactory explanations for why people leave the profession. Satisfaction is generally high. Nearly 90 percent of all professionals report being satisfied with the decision to obtain degrees or training in student personnel (Holmes, Verrier, and Chisholm, 1983). Optimism about or satisfaction with career goals characterizes most professionals, with nearly two-thirds indicating optimism (Bender, 1980; Grant and Foy, 1972; Holmes, Verrier, and Chisholm, 1983).

Paradoxically, the same professionals who reported satisfaction and optimism about career goals were likely to indicate that they did not intend to stay in the profession. In one study (Holmes, Verrier, and Chisholm, 1983), only 20 percent indicated that they planned to work in student affairs for their entire careers. Consistently, women tended to be a bit less satisfied with their careers and more likely to indicate that the profession did not fit them for their entire careers (Bender, 1980).

This paradox becomes a bit less mystifying if some other findings are considered. Nearly 100 percent of professionals viewed their jobs as important (Bender, 1980), but only 50 percent believed that others on campus saw them as important. Also, nearly 50 percent reported little respect for the chief student affairs officer. Do these data explain the contradiction of the finding that most people were satisfied with career goals but did not expect to stay? How long can one work in a career that interested one originally because of its service dimensions, when one does not think others see it as important? How long can one stay when one is dissatisfied with the leadership? Undoubtedly, these findings do not explain the paradox completely, but they do have implications for professional education and renewal needs.

Turnover among chief student affairs officers is about on a par with comparable administrative positions. Between 1974 and 1981, the total turnover rate was 100 percent; that is, the total changes were equal to or greater than the total number of positions (Rickard, 1982). Yearly turnover rate was about 17 percent, compared to 20 percent for academic officers, 16 percent for business officers, and 12 percent for institutional chief officers.

Despite this turnover, mobility among chief student officers may be decreasing a bit. Average age and average total years of experience seem to be rising. Average age has been about forty; several studies have reported it as high as forty-six (Paul and Hoover, 1980), and other studies have reported that between 58 percent and 76 percent were between thirty and fifty (Gross, 1978). Years of experience also have risen, with early studies indicating that fewer than half had been in the profession ten years or more (Brooks and Avila, 1974) and more recent studies suggesting that nearly two-thirds had been in the profession ten years or more (Harder, 1983; Paul and Hoover, 1980). Recent studies also indicate that more officers report that they plan to stay in their current positions (Harder, 1983).

What Are the Opportunities for Women and Minorities?

There is very little research on the subject of career paths or career status of minorities—so little that it is impossible to characterize the career status of minorities. The available research about women points to the conclusion that women remain underrepresented among the major administrative positions in student affairs. Women make up less than or only slightly more than 10 percent of the administrator population. In his compilation of studies, Gross (1978) found that between 82 percent and 100 percent of administrators were men. The same pattern held for director positions (81 percent to 91 percent men as counseling directors, 78 percent to 88 percent men as financial aid directors). Other positions, however, such as residence hall staff, placement staff, and activities staff, were more equally divided between men and women. Some signs point toward progress for women, however; new position openings are being filled about equally by men and women (Gross, 1978), and appointments of women and minorities to such positions as director of admissions have increased in the past several years (Rickard and Clement, 1984). Some indicators suggest that this trend represents a conscious policy of institutions, as women are more likely to be younger and to have spent less time in chief student affairs positions than men (Evans and Kuh, 1983; Rickard, 1985a; Rickard, 1985b). It is noteworthy that more women than men have degrees in college student personnel or related areas, but it is also distressing to find that more women are deans, while men are more likely to be vice-presidents (probably because there are more women chief officers at smaller institutions; see Evans and Kuh, 1983). At this time, women and minorities have made progress but still tend to hold lower positions (Welty, 1982).

Conclusions from the Research

These studies suggest several conclusions, some more tentative than others. First, there is no clear path to the top, if the top is defined as the position of chief student affairs officer. A doctorate seems to be a standard expectation, especially at larger institutions. Most officers have had prior administrative experience, either as generalists or as directors of student affairs divisions. Second, the field is still dominated by white males. Several indicators suggest that this may be changing, but the data are perhaps still too fluid to indicate a stable trend toward greater representation of either women or minorities in top leadership positions. For women, at least the trend is in the direction of greater equity. Third, fewer openings are expected in the next decade (Rickard, 1985b). As the number of students decreases, positions may be consolidated. Indications are that current administrators are more likely to stay longer in their current roles.

Results of studies of career paths for specific student affairs agencies present the same general pattern, with minor variations. Admissions officers (Chapman and Urbach, 1984) and financial aid directors (Galvez and Olinsky, 1980) become directors on the strength of a master's degree, but without the doctorate, movement is lateral. Small-college officers often have more experience in student affairs than do those in larger colleges and obtain top positions sooner (Kuh, Evans, and Duke, 1983).

Most studies on career pathways are really status profiles, rather than career-path or career-pattern studies. They provide snapshots of how many women or minorities are employed, or what age, experience, and training levels are like; but they do not provide a direct sense of movement. We get to see where the travelers are on the road (an external journey), but we do not see where they want to go or wanted to go (an internal journey). Researchers have spent a lot of effort looking at the supposed "top" of the profession and perhaps have presented the faulty and unsound impression that everyone wants to reach that point. This is rather strange for academia, because we do not make the same assumption for faculty: No one assumes that all faculty want to be department chairs, college deans, or presidents.

Career-Path Scenarios

Research studies with aggregate percentages, means, and standard deviations are helpful in obtaining some sense about the profession as a whole, but they help us understand neither our own development nor what is happening among the colleagues in the next office. These are the human stories that describe what it is like to be in student affairs—to be on the move upward, or to be trying to cope with long-lasting stability. Here are two sets of scenarios that may put more meaning into the data.

Vice-Chancellor Candidates. The research suggests several career-path scenarios. If we were reviewing the applications of candidates for vice-chancellor for student affairs, we might find the following applicants among those nominated.

1. John majored in history as an undergraduate, with certification as a secondary school teacher. He went to graduate school after obtaining his B.A. because he had a scholarship, but instead of going on in history, he decided to go on in guidance and counseling. After teaching high school history for two years, he worked at a small college as a career counselor. Eventually he got a Ph.D. in counseling and became director of counseling, first at a small college and later at a larger institution. He has been director for five years.

2. Steve started out as a student assistant in housing. After earning his B.A., he decided to work as a residence director at a small college while he went to graduate school in student personnel. This move led to his becoming assistant director of housing at a larger institution, where he enrolled and graduated from a higher education–student personnel program. He has been director of housing for six years since obtaining his Ph.D.

3. Sarah went to a small college and was active in campus activities. After encouragement from a woman counselor, she enrolled in graduate school in educational psychology, with a specialization in counseling. She worked for several years at a small college after obtaining her master's

degree. She returned to graduate school and several years later became assistant to the dean and then assistant vice-chancellor.

4. Harry received all his degrees in engineering. While teaching at one institution, he gained a reputation as an excellent advisor and eventually became assistant dean of the college of engineering. For the past three years he has been dean of students at a moderate-sized institution.

All four could easily be viable candidates for vice-chancellor. None of them would be a "surprise" appointment, given the current backgrounds of chief student affairs officers across the country.

Professionals Without Hope for the Top. Most career-path research has focused on applicants for (or people in positions as) chief student affairs officer. Another set of people on many campuses, however, has been largely neglected by researchers. Let us look at scenarios that include them.

1. James has been at a counseling center for fifteen years. He obtained his Ph.D. in counseling psychology and has been employed at the counseling center ever since. He had some prior experience as a high school counselor and at a mental health center. He has had an adjunct appointment with the doctoral counseling program on campus and advises students on occasion. He also teaches one course per semester. He vacillates between trying to become the counseling center's director and becoming a full-time faculty member. The current director is entrenched, however. Moreover, because of family ties, James is not too eager to change locations. His research record is not strong enough to become a full-time faculty member in his academic department.

2. Joan has been director of financial aid on campus for six years. She was one of the first women administrators on campus. She is getting burned out by the continual ups and downs of financial aid, not knowing from one year to the next how much money will be available. There are always new regulations to learn, interpret, and apply. Her background was originally in business management. She does not see much room or hope for advancement; the current administration seems satisfied with the number of women in administration and views her abilities and position rather narrowly. She thinks seriously from time to time about leaving higher education to enter business, but that world seems remote—as remote as advancement in student affairs.

3. Peter has been assistant director of campus activities for six years. He is black and about forty years old. He entered student affairs as a minority recruiter and then became a minority counselor in a division focusing on minority programming and student needs. That division was disbanded, and Peter was given the opportunity to work in campus activities. He is the only minority staff member in campus activities and therefore tends to work almost exclusively with minority students. There does not seem to be much room to go anywhere. He sees his work as an important

service for minority students, but he is not sure how much he is valued by his colleagues.

4. Susan has been a residence hall director for five years. She has a master's degree in student personnel and "grew up" professionally in the residence halls. She was a student assistant on the same campus where she is now a residence director. She did all her academic work at the same institution. She feels recognized as a competent professional, but she is tired of the live-in situation; it has substantially inhibited her social life. Currently, there are no positions open in residence education. She debates whether to apply for a position elsewhere. That seems as if it would be her best option if she were to make a vertical move.

These scenarios are also not unusual and probably typify many campuses. Here are four competent individuals with no need to move either toward the chief student affairs position or necessarily toward higher positions in their own specialties. Yet somehow they do not seem to themselves professionally complete. They are not severely burned out; it is just that there is no place to go.

Implications for Professional Education Programming and Research

Reviews of research literature often end with suggestions for programming and for further research. Usually these are declarative statements, distinct from one other. The body of knowledge on career paths of student affairs professionals is not of sufficient depth or quality to warrant such directives. Instead, the implications for programming must be tentative and subjected to further research. These implications are phrased, for this reason, as questions, rather than as suggestions.

1. We need an analytical examination of the meaning of the attrition research. Studies indicate a relatively high attrition rate, especially among women professionals. Is this something to be concerned about? Some authors suggest that it is, because high attrition both indicates low morale and demands constant training of new professionals. Others suggest that high attrition provides the opportunity for a constant supply of new blood that revitalizes student services. Should professional education efforts focus on preventing attrition, or should they emphasize sharpening and updating the skills of the stayers?

2. We need a redefinition of success. To be a complete professional, does one have to become a chief student affairs officer? Despite a nearly 20 percent annual turnover rate, most prognosticators suggest that openings will be scarcer in the future. Not everyone can be at the top; success has to be defined as doing one's professional best. How should success be defined? What are the implications for training programs and for working with staff members who will be in the same positions for the rest of their

careers? (The professional education model in Chapter Two helps to alter our perceptions of professional success and development.)

3. What model should we use for understanding career development of student personnel professionals? Most research thus far has been atheoretical and has involved survey methodology. Often the return rates are quite modest. The work of Carpenter and Miller (1981) is a beginning look at the career-path question from a developmental perspective. Can we implement our theories of human development among our own professional ranks, as well as with our students (Arnold, 1982)? Can we develop and test a model that incorporates the development of minorities?

4. How can we rejuvenate professionals who have no opportunity to advance and who may have no desire to relocate? What will work? Job rotation? Mentoring programs? Monitoring burnout?

5. Professional education needs cut across all levels and affect the vice-chancellor as well as the new residence hall staff member. The rapid expansion of theoretical and empirical support for education programming may already have bypassed many in major administrative positions. How do we keep the professionals current, when new blood will perhaps not be accessible? We need a model for professional education that considers developmental stages and age levels, one that will provide a framework for planning programs and interventions that will meet individual staff needs. (The model outlined in Chapter Two has that potential.)

Endnotes: References and Rhetoric

It is customary to end a chapter with rhetoric that inspires everyone to go forth and change the world, or at least his or her own campus. I have been as guilty of that as anyone else. I would like to end this chapter a bit more concretely by briefly noting two studies that warrant special consideration as potential models for further research. One is by Carpenter and Miller (1981), and the other is by Wood, Winston, and Polkosnik (1985).

Carpenter and Miller (1981) designed an instrument, the Student Affairs Professional Development Inventory (SAPDI) to assess development stages with forty-nine items related to professional development tasks. In this investigation, they randomly surveyed professionals and found administrators scoring higher than counselors, older professionals higher than young professionals, single women higher than single men, and married men higher than married women. There were no significant differences among members of different professional organizations.

Wood, Winston, and Polkosnik (1985) built on the Carpenter and Miller study. They used a Career Orientations Inventory (DeLong, 1981) and the SAPDI to look at professional development stages and career orientation, as they relate to persistence in student affairs careers. They reported that professionals with broad interest in the field, with moderate interest in expertise in one or more program or service areas, with a low need for variety, and with a willingness to relocate were most likely to reach the generative professional development stage. Those who left the profession tended to be those with higher needs for autonomy, coupled with lower needs to stay in the same geographical regions.

These studies are highlighted less because of their specific findings than because of their approaches to the research questions. They started with theoretically premised questions, looked at career paths from a developmental perspective, sought to obtain psychological and sociological information along with other demographic data, and used appropriate methodologies to examine their research questions. Although relying heavily on survey methods, with the usual problems regarding return rates, these kinds of studies serve as models for future research on career-path explorations.

Readers eager to have ideas for implementing professional education efforts at the local campus, regional, or national levels will get some helpful ideas from the Carpenter and Miller and Wood, Winston, and Polkosnik studies. Currently, however, until the body of knowledge increases in depth and sophistication, planners will do just as well to look at the conceptual literature that raises questions about what the profession needs to be like in the future. Stamatakos and Rogers (1984) suggest that we need a sense of philosophy. Kelly (1984) suggests that we need more mentoring. Kuh (1984) indicates that we need to be able to take a multiple perspective, using anthropology, organizational theory, and other approaches. Shaffer (1984) calls for more program evaluation skills. These are just a few of the available suggestions. Most of all, these efforts must help to provide a sense of professionalism among student affairs staff who may not be able or who may not want to reach what we have perhaps inappropriately called the "top."

The lack of useful and high-quality research on professional pathways does not mean that we should ignore the current literature, for it has some use. It does demand, however, that we move forward by conducting research that is theory-based and conceptually sound. (Rhetoric, at last!)

References

Arnold, K. "Career Development for the Experienced Student Affairs Professional." *National Association of Student Personnel Administrators Journal*, 1982, *20* (2), 3–8.

Bender, B. "Job Satisfaction in Student Affairs." *National Association of Student Personnel Administrators Journal*, 1980, *18* (2), 2–9.

Brooks, G., and Avila, J. "The Chief Student Personnel Administrator and His Staff: A Profile." *National Association of Student Personnel Administrators Journal*, 1974, *11* (4), 41–47.

Burns, M. "Who Leaves the Student Affairs Field?" *National Association of Student Personnel Administrators Journal,* 1982, *20* (2), 4-12.

Carpenter, D. S., and Miller, T. K. "An Analysis of Professional Development in Student Affairs Work." *National Association of Student Personnel Administrators Journal,* 1981, *19,* 2-11.

Chapman, D., and Urbach, S. "Career Paths of College Admissions Directors." *National Association of Student Personnel Administrators Journal,* 1984, *25* (1), 61-68.

DeLong, T. "A Comparison of the Career Orientation of Rural and Urban Educators." *Education Review,* 1981, *4* (1), 67-74.

Evans, N., and Kuh, G. "Getting to the Top: A Profile of the Female CSAO." *Journal of the National Association of Women Deans, Administrators, and Counselors,* 1983, *46* (3), 18-22.

Galvez, M., and Olinsky, A. "Financial Aid Administrators—Who Are They and What Are Their Training Needs? *Journal of Student Financial Aid,* 1980, *10,* 29-33.

Grant, W., and Foy, J. "Career Patterns of Student Personnel Administrators." *National Association of Student Personnel Administrators Journal,* 1972, *10,* 106-113.

Gross, S. "Characteristics of Student Personnel Workers: A Review of the Research." *Journal of College Student Personnel,* 1978, *19,* 231-237.

Harder, M. "Career Patterns of Chief Student Personnel Administrators." *Journal of College Student Personnel,* 1983, *24,* 443-448.

Holmes, D., Verrier, D., and Chisholm, P. "Persistence in Student Affairs Work: Attitudes and Job Shifts Among Master's Program Graduates." *Journal of College Student Personnel,* 1983, *24,* 439-443.

Hoyt, D., and Tripp, P. "Characteristics of ACPA Members." *Journal of College Student Personnel,* 1967, *8,* 32-39.

Kelly, K. "Initiating a Relationship with a Mentor in Student Affairs." *National Association of Student Personnel Administrators Journal,* 1984, *21,* 49-54.

Kuh, G. "A Framework for Understanding Student Affairs Work." *Journal of College Student Personnel,* 1984, *25,* 25-31.

Kuh, G., Evans, N., and Duke, A. "Career Paths and Responsibilities of CSAOs." *National Association of Student Personnel Administrators Journal,* 1983, *21,* 39-47.

Lawing, M., Moore, L., and Groseth, R. "Enhancement and Advancement: Professional Development for Student Affairs Staff." *National Association of Student Personnel Administrators Journal,* 1982, *20* (2), 22-26.

Lunsford, L. "Chief Student Affairs Officers Influence the Ladder to the Top." *National Association of Student Personnel Administrators Journal,* 1984, *22* (1), 48-56.

Moore, L., and Burns, M. "Recruiting the Entry-Level Professional and the Middle Manager in Student Affairs." *Journal of College and University Student Housing,* 1983, *13,* 19-23.

Ostroth, D., Efird, F., and Lerman, L. "Career Patterns of Chief Student Affairs Officers." *Journal of College Student Personnel,* 1984, *25,* 443-448.

Paul, W., and Hoover, R. "Chief Student Personnel Administrators: A Decade of Change." *National Association of Student Personnel Administrators Journal,* 1980, *18* (1), 33-39.

Rickard, S. "Turnover at the Top: A Study of the CSAO." *National Association of Student Personnel Administrators Journal,* 1982, *20* (2), 36-41.

Rickard, S. "A Career Pathway of Chief Student Affairs Officers: Making Room at the Top for Women and Minorities." *National Association of Student Personnel Administrators Journal,* 1985a, *22* (4), 52-60.

Rickard, S. "The Chief Student Affairs Officer: Progress Toward Equity." *Journal of College Student Personnel,* 1985b, *26,* 5-10.

Rickard, S., and Clement, L. "The Director of Admissions: Progress Toward Equity for Women and Minorities." *Journal of College Admissions,* 1984, *104,* 24-27.

Shaffer, R. "Critical Dimensions of Student Affairs in the Decades Ahead." *Journal of College Student Personnel,* 1984, *25,* 112-114.

Stamatakos, L., and Rogers, R. "Student Affairs: A Profession in Need of a Philosophy." *Journal of College Student Personnel,* 1984, *25,* 400-411.

Welty, J. "Minorities in Housing Administration." *The Journal of College and University Student Housing,* 1982, *12,* 31-33.

Wood, L., Winston, R., and Polkosnik, M. "Career Orientation and Professional Development of Young Student Affairs Professionals." *Journal of College Student Personnel,* 1985, *26,* 532-539.

Robert D. Brown is professor of educational psychology at the University of Nebraska-Lincoln and editor of the Journal of College Student Personnel.

This chapter relates professional education to the professional status of student affairs and includes a model of professional education to involve different educational modes, types of practice, and career stages.

A Model of Professional Education

Robert B. Young

What is a profession? It is not a business, a science, or a racket (Becker, 1956). A profession is an occupation with dignity. The label connotes full-time devotion among the employees in that occupation and the notion that they possess special proficiency (Pavalko, 1971). The dignity of the term is more secure than its definition. Hundreds of definitions have been offered for *profession* since 1915, some broad and some narrowly restricted (Houle, 1981).

Although the definitions differ, only one method is usually used to determine the professional status of an occupation: Criteria are measured against practice. The criteria might differ; the assessments might, too; but this method of determining professional status has been maintained for almost fifty years (Houle, 1981).

Just what are the criteria for determining whether or not an occupation is a profession? Wrenn and Darley (1949) identified the following:

- The application of standards of selection and training
- The possession of a body of specialized knowledge and skills
- The development of a professional consciousness and of professional groups
- The self-imposition of standards of admission and performance
- The definition of job titles and functions

L. V. Moore, R. B. Young (eds.). *Expanding Opportunities for Professional Education.*
New Directions for Student Services, no. 37. San Francisco: Jossey-Bass, Spring 1987.

- The legal recognition of the vocation
- The performance of a socially needed function
- High moral and personal integrity and the development of a code of ethics.

Greenwood (1957) identifies five similar criteria:

- A systematic body of theory, which affects professional skills and training
- Sanctions of the professional community through licensing, accreditation, and privileged communication
- A professional culture
- Professional authority
- A regulative code of ethics.

Implicit in these criteria is the notion that professions have a responsibility to educate their members, both as an entry requirement and as a continuing professional responsibility. The first four criteria identified by Wrenn and Darley and the first three identified by Greenwood are related to professional education. Thus, professional education is very strongly linked to the requirements of a profession.

Although there has been considerable discussion about the professional status of student affairs (Stamatakos, 1981), the practitioners and associations of the field assume it is professional, requiring appropriate behaviors and attitudes. (Thus, a major assumption of this sourcebook is that student affairs is a profession and, as such, includes professional education as one of its primary attributes.)

Definitional problems affect a discussion of professional education. For the purposes of this sourcebook, the umbrella term *professional education* refers to the introduction and continual updating of theory, skills, and perspectives of student affairs practitioners. This is accomplished through formal and informal means, which can range from graduate programs to telephone contacts with colleagues. In this sourcebook, the terms *graduate education, continuing education, in-service education, staff development, in-service training,* and others are often used interchangeably to refer to methods of delivering professional education.

Of the various ways in which professional education is implemented, graduate programs are typically the first step in professional education for persons entering the student affairs profession. Professional education after formal graduate education is usually concurrent with employment and includes any efforts to update theory, skills, and perspectives.

The Need for a Model of Expanded Professional Education

Unfortunately, it's easier to talk about professional education than to do something about it. Houle (1981) has been a severe critic of the "mindless proliferation" of courses and conferences, which are not unified by a conception of professional education. In Chapter One, Brown indicates that conceptual incoherence marks professional education in student affairs, and he calls for models and studies based on theory to provide a conceptual basis for graduate education programs and meet the needs of practitioners.

The remainder of this chapter is devoted to the presentation and elaboration of a model of expanded professional education in student affairs. The model was developed by Leila V. Moore and Robert B. Young. We hope that this model will help student affairs professionals to understand professional education and to determine what kinds of professional education experiences student affairs organizations should develop.

Figure 1 displays the model of professional education for student affairs. This model attempts to define professional education by identifying relationships among (1) stages of professional development of the student affairs practitioner, (2) types of interpersonal relationships encountered by the practitioner on the job, and (3) modes of education appropriate to practitioners.

Stages of Professional Development. According to Carpenter (1980), human development theory helps explain the professional development of student affairs workers. His model of professional development contains formative, application, and additive stages. Carpenter (1980) and Young (1985) have noted some similarity between these career stages and the Eriksonian stages of identity, intimacy, and generativity. The professional development of student affairs practitioners might be a subset of general human development, related to age as much as to a particular field of employment.

The *formative stage* usually involves students in master's degree programs, who have chosen student affairs as a profession but lack professional experience and training. Although graduate education is emphasized at this stage, Carpenter contends that formative practitioners need a model of expanded professional education; otherwise, they will be handicapped later.

During the *application stage,* new practitioners gain on-the-job supervision and commit themselves to careers in student affairs. This stage ends with the decision to seek further education or increased job responsibilities.

The *additive stage* involves policymakers who represent the interests of the field on and off campus. They might become mentors, transmitting to others their commitment to and knowledge of the field. In turn, they might replenish their own commitment and knowledge through lifelong learning.

The Carpenter model can be used in situational as well as absolute ways. While the stages form a general career sequence for most student affairs administrators and counselors, they also are recycled at different times in an individual's career. For example, an additive career person might be a "formative" chief student affairs officer upon the assumption

Figure 1. A Model of Professional Education for Student Affairs Staff

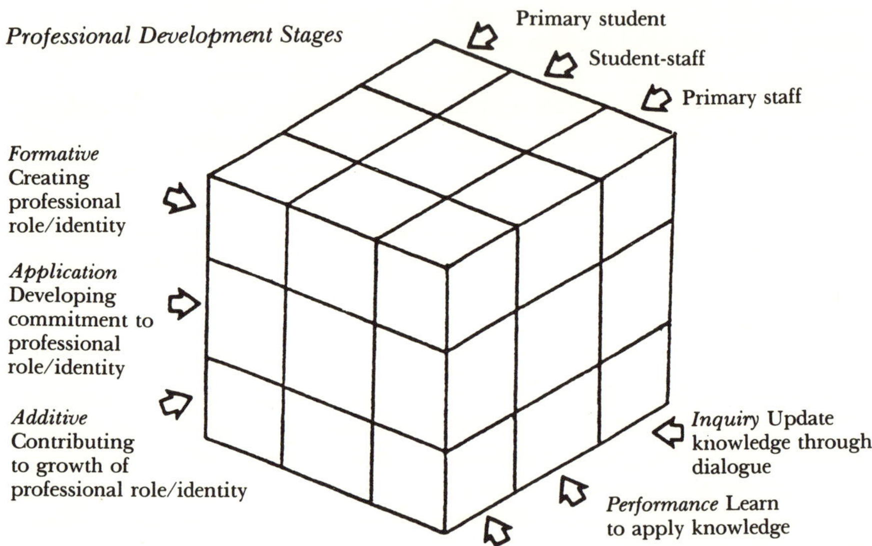

of those duties. This practitioner might need basic instruction about that position at the same time that he or she is contributing to the literature of the field. Bloland (1979) says that chief student affairs officers need different instruction as general administrators than entry practitioners need as human development specialists.

Types of Interpersonal Relationships. A comprehensive model of professional education must also include different career types, to alter the equation of administrative advancement with professional maturation. Those career types might be classified by the relationships that student affairs professionals encounter on the job, including primarily *student-centered, student/staff-centered,* or *staff-centered.*

A classification according to these relationships makes sense, since interpersonal contacts are so significant in the student affairs profession. Interpersonal skills are the most important criterion for employment in the field (Ostroth, 1981; Roberts and Keys, 1983), and interpersonal contacts dominate daily activities.

The differentiation among primarily student-centered, student/

staff–centered, and staff-centered relationships accommodates a variety of student affairs professional positions. For example, it takes into account the residence director and the psychologist who spend most of their time with students; the program director who spends equal time with students and staff; the chief student affairs officer of a small college who has as much student as staff contact; and the vice-chancellor of a multiversity who has moved from student-centered to student/staff–centered to staff-centered positions.

Modes of Education for Professionals. Houle (1981) describes three types of education for professionals: instruction, performance, and inquiry. Instruction concerns the dissemination of professional knowledge, skills, or sensitivity. It is usually associated with graduate classroom education more than with in-service training.

Performance concerns the internalization of work concepts and the application of professional practices. Although it is a part of graduate education, it dominates on-the-job education. Gross and Osterman (1972) contend that performance education deserves greater prominence in educational activities for professionals, since instruction is excessively prolonged.

Inquiry concerns the integration of ideas, techniques, policies, and strategies into professional fields. It overcomes the limits of classroom and practical learning (Chenault and Burnford, 1978). Inquiry is often stimulated by professional association activities—for example, when practitioners and educators gather to discuss and amend professional philosophy and practices.

All three modes of education for professionals are familiar to student affairs practitioners. Professional preparation programs offer instruction in the classroom setting and performance learning through practice and internships. Instruction can also appear in continuing professional education. For example, the Generativity Project of the American College Personnel Association includes a compilation of videotapes about issues in higher education. Performance education appears in on-the-job training, mentoring relationships, accreditation visits, job evaluations, and simulation training models. Inquiry occurs whenever two administrators from different colleges talk about their job concerns, perhaps at national, regional, or staff association conferences. Inquiry might also be promoted through interactive video, retreats, institutes, and professional education centers (such as the one described in Chapter Six).

In summary, this comprehensive model allows practitioners to conceptualize, perhaps for the first time, professional education in a way that takes into account the interaction of their stages of professional development, the focus on their interpersonal relationships, and appropriate modes of education. This model also allows for the selection of professional education activities that are relevant to the individual professional and appropriate to the needs of student affairs organizations.

Using The Model

This model can be used by individuals, as well as by student affairs organizations, graduate programs, and professional associations for assessing, receiving, or delivering professional education.

Individuals. This model can help individuals discover their immediate and long-range professional education needs and the means for meeting those needs. In Chapter Three, Moore develops a structured interview, based on the model, that can be used to help individual practitioners do just that.

Institutions. Managers of student affairs organizations can use this model to determine the professional education needs of their employees and to develop in-service training programs that integrate employee needs with institutional goals.

Graduate Programs. Graduate programs might use this model to assess their curricula, courses, and modes of education, so that the needs of their graduate students can be integrated into the instructional goals of their programs.

Professional Associations. Professional associations can use this model to develop themes for national and regional conventions and workshops and to stimulate discussions and debate about professional education in student affairs.

Summary and Conclusions

In this chapter, I have argued that professional education is a required part of the activity of a profession. The student affairs profession needs a model to help practitioners and educators conceptualize professional education in a way that meets institutional and individual needs. A model of professional education, based on the educational concepts of Houle (1981), was presented. It takes into account (1) the stages of professional development of student affairs practitioners, (2) the types of interpersonal relationships of these practitioners, and (3) the modes of education appropriate to professional education.

References

Becker, H. S. "Some Problems of Professionalism." *Adult Education,* 1956, *6,* 101–105.

Bloland, P. "Student Personnel Training for the Chief Student Affairs Officer: Essential or Unnecessary?" *NASPA Journal,* 1979, *17,* 57–62.

Carpenter, D. "The Professional Development of Student Personnel Workers: An Analysis." Unpublished doctoral dissertation, University of Georgia, 1980.

Chenault, J., and Burnford, F. *Human Services Professional Education.* New York: McGraw-Hill, 1978.

Greenwood, E. "Attributes of a Profession." *Social Work*, 1957, *2*, 45–55.

Gross, R., and Osterman, P. (eds.). *The New Professionals*. New York: Simon & Schuster, 1972.

Houle, C. *Continuing Learning in the Professions*. San Francisco: Jossey-Bass, 1981.

Ostroth, D. "Competencies for Entry-Level Professionals: What Do Employers Look For When Hiring New Staff?" *Journal of College Student Personnel*, 1981, *22*, 5–11.

Pavalko, R. *Sociological Perspectives on Occupations*. Itasca, Ill.: Peacock, 1971.

Roberts, D., and Keys, A. "Student Personnel Hiring Practices." Paper presented at the meeting of the American College Personnel Association, Houston, March 1983.

Stamatakos, L. "Student Affairs Progress Toward Professionalism: Recommendations for Action." *Journal of College Student Personnel*, 1981, *22*, 105–112 and 197–206.

Wrenn, C., and Darley, J. "Appraisal of the Professional Status of Student Personnel Work." In E. G. Williamson (ed.), *Trends in Student Personnel Work*. Minneapolis: University of Minnesota, 1949.

Young, R. "Impressions of the Development of Professional Identity: From Program to Practice." *NASPA Journal*, 1985, *23*, 50–60.

Robert B. Young is associate professor and program adviser for higher education administration and coordinator of faculty development for the College of Education at Kent State University.

*The model of expanded professional education might
be used in two ways: for individual assessment and
prescription and for institutional program development.*

Using the Model of Expanded Professional Education

Leila V. Moore

There are three basic uses for a model of expanded professional education. First, a model provides a method for identifying the professional development levels of student affairs staff and facilitating recommendations for learning activities appropriate to those levels. Second, it provides a method of planning for the professional education of staff at all levels within an institution. Finally, it identifies gaps in the programs and structures of professional education within the entire field of student affairs. This chapter includes a discussion of the first two uses; Chapter Seven involves the third basic use of the model.

In Chapter Two, Young has presented a three-dimensional model of expanded professional education. The model includes (1) types of professional employment, based on proportion of contact between students and staff; (2) levels of professional development, ranging from learning about work *(formative)* to forming a commitment to the field *(application)* to transmitting knowledge to others *(additive)*; and (3) modes of education, including classroom *(instruction)*, on-the-job *(performance)* and seminar forms of learning *(inquiry)*.

Working with Individual Staff

In working with individual staff, one would use the model to diagnose the current developmental needs and interests of a staff member and

L. V. Moore, R. B. Young (eds.). *Expanding Opportunities for Professional Education.*
New Directions for Student Services, no. 37. San Francisco: Jossey-Bass, Spring 1987.

then to prescribe an educational program for that staff member. The steps involved in using the model with individual staff are presented below. (A summary of the interview protocol for each assessment step is found in the appendix to this sourcebook.)

Diagnosing Individual Level and Prescribing Activities. In the first part of an assessment, an interviewer asks the staff member to estimate the proportion of current work time spent with students and staff (including faculty). The answer is categorized either as spending the majority of time with students, spending about equal time with staff and students, or spending the majority of time with staff. The staff member declares whether he or she wants to maintain or change this ratio in the next stage of his or her career.

Next, the interviewer asks the staff member to discuss his or her professional development. The staff member indicates length of his or her full-time employment and length of time in the current position. In addition, the staff member responds to several questions about mentoring—whether he or she has a mentor now, wants a mentor, or serves as a mentor for other staff members.

Educational experiences are assessed next. The staff member identifies the main benefits that were derived from his or her last professional education activity. Following this is a discussion of the benefits derived from the latest attendance at a national or regional conference. Formal education is also assessed, including dates of advanced degrees, current enrollment in graduate classes, and (if applicable) benefits of those classes. Finally, the staff member assesses his or her opportunities to grow professionally in the present job, including the aspects of that job that he or she would enhance or change in order to make the total position more attractive.

After the interviewer gathers this information, he or she places the staff member on each of the three dimensions of the professional education model. At the same time, the staff member makes an independent assessment about his or her own placement on each of the dimensions. Disparities in perception are reviewed, and consensus is reached about the placement.

Once consensus is reached, the model is used to make recommendations for the professional education of the student affairs staff member. Suggestions emerge from the level above the staff member on the dimensions of mode of education and professional development. If any aspects of the staff member's current or former level seem undeveloped or missing, recommendations for filling in the gaps are also suggested. The desired ratio of staff-student contact guides additional recommendations for professional education activities.

Field-Testing the Model with Individuals. This interview protocol was tested in November and December of 1985 with twenty-five staff members from two universities. In 80 percent of the tests, the interviewer and the staff member agreed about placement on all three dimensions of the model. In the remaining cases, the differences in placement affected only one dimension of the model. The differences were attributed to career transitions for the staff member, from one developmental level to another.

The five vignettes that follow illustrate the use of the interview protocol with the professional education model.

Anne. Anne is twenty-five years old and a residence staff member. She supervises four other full-time and two clerical staff members. She has just enrolled in a doctoral program in college student personnel, and she expects to finish the degree part-time within five years. During the week, Anne spends about an equal amount of time with staff and with students. She has no mentor now, although she stops in to see a staff member in the student affairs office from time to time. She would like to develop a mentor relationship with that person.

Anne expects to remain in her current position until she finishes her degree. She wishes she had more time on the job to devote to group work with students, and she wishes she could participate in one university-wide committee, just for the exposure to the campus. The last national conference she attended was her first national meeting. She observed other presenters there, and she hopes to present a program herself at the next national meeting she attends. She has been a presenter at a regional meeting, an experience she enjoyed very much.

On the professional education model, Anne is in a position that affords equal amounts of staff and student contact. She is at the application level on the professional development dimension and at the performance level on the dimension of educational modes. These recommendations are made for Anne's professional education activities:

1. Develop the mentor relationship with the staff member in the student affairs office. This seems to be an unfinished piece of business from the formative stage of her professional development dimension.

2. Develop a proposal for a presentation at a national conference, in order to expand experience with inquiry education and organize performance learning.

3. Volunteer to teach one of the undergraduate courses in career decision making at her institution, as a way to add more performance learning.

4. Locate a counseling center staff member and a faculty member who would be willing to supervise her coursework and training as a facilitator for personal-growth groups. This builds mentoring relationships, instruction modes, and student-contact skills.

5. Let her supervisor know about her specific interests in university-wide committee work, to enhance staff contact and performance learning.

Frank. Frank is forty-five years old and a senior student affairs staff member. He has a doctorate in college student personnel, and he has worked full-time for the last twenty-five years. He has held his current position for four years. Frank spends most of his work week in contact with staff and faculty at the university. He would like to become a vice-president for student affairs, but he does not expect to move up until his children finish high school, five years from now.

Frank reports general dissatisfaction with regional and national conventions. He wishes he could find affordable intensive seminars to attend, where the groups are small and where he could really learn about financial management. He wants time to talk with other deans and vice-presidents, to learn about their perspectives and experiences.

On the job, Frank wishes he could motivate his staff more and that he had constructive feedback from his supervisor on how he might improve. Frank reports that he has never had a mentor, although he has been a mentor for some graduate students.

Frank is in a staff-centered position on the model of professional education. His professional needs are additive within his present position, even though he has never had a mentor. Inquiry is his dominant mode of professional education, and national and regional associations are not meeting Frank's needs for this type of education.

Professional education possibilities for Frank include:

1. Find and attend national seminars or institutes on financial management. This is a staff-centered skill, which Frank needs now and will also need later as a vice-president for student affairs.

2. Utilize national conferences for colleagueship, if not for formal learning. More than the sessions, utilize the informal opportunities for inquiry learning at these conferences. Meet with chief student affairs officers, forming a network of professional colleagues who can assist with a future job search.

3. Locate a mentor within the above network to satisfy that need. Frank needs this type of colleague to help him assess his qualifications and plans to be a chief student affairs officer.

4. Attend to younger full-time professional staff members on campus, establishing at least one mentor relationship there, so that Frank satisfies the additive requirements of his current position.

5. Evaluate the need for instruction in financial management, even though classroom instruction is not the dominant mode of education for Frank.

6. Sharpen supervision and management skills by seeking feedback from his supervisor and by locating on-campus committees or special projects that contribute to these skills. These staff-contact skills are necessary for Frank's current and anticipated work.

Eleanor. Eleanor is thirty-nine years old. She has recently changed careers, from a position in a local counseling agency to her current job as director of a student affairs function. Eleanor supervises a staff of three professionals and a secretary. She has a doctorate in clinical psychology.

Eleanor has had twelve years of experience as a therapist, has served as a mentor to younger psychologists, and has been fairly active at the state and regional levels of several mental health organizations. However, her new position requires knowledge of organizations, of the dynamics of change, and of the role of consultant to other staff in working with students. These areas are new to her.

Eleanor spends just over 50 percent of her time with students, another 35 percent with staff or faculty, and the balance on paperwork. She wants to acquire the knowledge required in her new position but is concerned that this will take time from her family. She and her husband have finally adjusted to Eleanor's new schedule, settled into a child-care routine, and found regular time for themselves. Eleanor is reluctant to disturb the schedule she and her family have created; she does not want to develop the "workaholic" patterns that she has seen in many other student affairs professionals. Eleanor does not expect to change jobs until her children graduate from high school.

On the professional education model, Eleanor is in a position that focuses on staff more than on students. In her new position, she has formative needs that require instruction as the dominant mode of education. She reports a strong need for a mentor in her new position.

Eleanor is also in the application stage within her general career development, and most of her education should occur in performance and inquiry modes. Thus, Eleanor's career reveals the limitations of a singular model of professional education. An application or additive professional, she feels that she should "regress" and that her family might suffer while she "plays catch-up" to meet the formative requirements of her new position. Given these considerations, professional education activities for Eleanor might include these options:

1. Increase time with staff and faculty by delegating more student contact to her staff. This would bring her ratio of time with staff and faculty into greater accord with the responsibilities of her job. It might also provide her with greater support during her period of adjustment to her new position.

2. Locate a series of seminars or workshops related to the skills of her new position and that offer intensive instruction in a compressed period of time (weekend workshops or one-day meetings). Schedule these opportunities around family time.

3. Rent or purchase audiotape cassettes of speeches or workshops, and play these while traveling to or from work or en route to seminars and workshops. These will provide instruction that will be useful later at inquiry-oriented seminars.

4. Attend national conventions as a participant, especially at sessions related to her job. During these conventions, develop a network with staff at other institutions who have similar job titles. Use the convention for "shop talk" with these individuals, who can meet Eleanor's multiple needs for mentoring, performance learning, and inquiry.

5. Find a person on campus with the knowledge base she needs and arrange a weekly two-hour luncheon to discuss topics related to this knowledge base.

Tony. Tony is the coordinator of programs for commuter students. He is thirty-one years old, and has a master's degree in psychology. He has held his current position for five years. This is Tony's first position in student affairs and his first full-time work experience. He is in a one-person office, and has not had the experience of supervising full-time or part-time staff at any level. He shares a secretary with the director of student life, who is his immediate supervisor. During the week, Tony spends about two-thirds of his time attending student programs or meeting individually with students. The remainder of his time is spent attending meetings with other staff and serving as adviser to the Black Student Caucus, a group whose purpose is to provide a positive campus atmosphere for black students. His work as an advisor to this group has been praised by many staff on campus, but has not become part of Tony's job description. Tony's supervisor is wholly supportive of his advisor role and seems pleased that Tony has made such a positive contribution.

Tony expects to remain in his current position for several more years. He expresses a concern that he needs to be doing more on the job, but is not sure what that might be. As a black staff member, and one of two black student affairs staff members, he sees a clear role for himself with black students. He values his associations with black students but feels that other white staff do not validate this association as part of his professional identity. Tony is not as clear about his role with commuter students and programs, but he reports that he has received very positive feedback about his work from both students and his supervisor. About his work with commuters, Tony attributes his success to luck. He does not consider himself a real professional because his degree is in psychology, rather than in student personnel.

Tony attends two conferences each year: one national student affairs meeting and one state meeting of black staff and faculty in higher education. He enjoys both meetings very much, both for the renewal that comes from getting away and gaining perspective and for the ideas he can bring back for use on his own campus. He has not presented a workshop or other program at a national student affairs meeting, but he is a frequent presenter at state meetings of black educators. Tony would like to offer a program at a national student affairs conference using some of the material he has presented to black educators, but he also expresses reluctance to do so.

On the professional education model, Tony is in a position with primarily student contacts. He seems to be at the formative professional development level in his work with the Black Student Caucus. Because of his focus on performance learning in the black educators' meetings, Tony seems ready for this type of learning activity. However, he seems to be in the instruction mode in terms of his expressed need for more knowledge about commuters. These recommendations are made for Tony:

1. Meet more frequently with his immediate supervisor to discuss needed support in his one-person office, his own professional goals, and the relationship of his work with black students to his current position. With his supervisor, Tony might:

- Identify specific aspects of his performance as coordinator of commuter programs that need improvement;
- Negotiate the inclusion of his work with the Black Student Caucus into his job description. (Here, Tony may need to be ready to explain the contribution he is making to the quality of campus life, including specific reference to the positive feedback he has received about his work.);
- Set performance goals—both for six months and for one year—that include his work with commuter and black students.

Increasing contact with his supervisor is intended to close the gap between the formative and applicative levels of Tony's professional development.

2. Develop a reading list on student development theory and enlist the assistance of a staff member with recent coursework in student development to discuss the readings in the context of commuter students. This activity responds to Tony's need for instruction in basic theory.

3. With the other black student affairs staff members, design a presentation on the role and contributions of black staff members to a predominately white student affairs staff. The topic could be presented first to the staff at Tony's university and perhaps later at a regional or national student affairs conference. This activity serves, again, to close the gap between Tony's two levels of development.

4. Locate a mentor who is black and who has succeeded in gaining institutional recognition and support for his or her dual responsibilities to student affairs and to the black community. A black mentor may be helpful to Tony in completing the formative stages of his professional identity.

Roberta. Roberta is a student aid officer. She is thirty-seven years old and recently widowed. She has two children, ages ten and twelve. Roberta supervises a staff of seven wage payroll clerks, a secretary, and four full-time professional staff. She has an MBA as well as a master's degree in college student personnel.

The recent death of her husband has complicated Roberta's career concerns considerably. Prior to his death, Roberta had been contemplating a job change to alumni affairs. She had identified a number of new responsibilities that she would enjoy, such as contacting alumni groups to update them on changes within the university; working with and learning from staff who have expertise in marketing, public relations, and fund raising; and working much more with staff than with students. As a result of her husband's death and the need for her to spend more time on child care, Roberta is no longer sure about making this change. She feels "stuck" in many ways now and reports that she is leaning on her friends to help her through this time.

Roberta has stopped attending national and regional conferences. She no longer gains benefit from them and is tired of being a presenter. She has no plans for further education. She reads widely, both in student aid and alumni affairs. She feels up-to-date as a student affairs professional. Her contributions to the entire university seem to satisfy her very much. She is proud of her appointments to several universitywide committees and has made a special point of her appointments to broadly based committees that are not focused specifically on student aid.

On the professional education model, Roberta is in a position with heavy student contact. However, with her added committee participation, her work days include a balance of student and staff contact. In terms of her professional development, she seems to be in the additive stage. Her comments suggest that she has developed a strong commitment to her profession and has already found satisfaction in the generative activities of the additive stage. Roberta is at the inquiry level in her preferred mode of learning. These activities are recommended for Roberta:

1. The shock of suddenly becoming a single parent and grieving her husband's death are still major forces in Roberta's life. She seems to be attending to the grieving process in a beneficial way. However, she might wish to talk with other staff members who are single parents and to her own children about her new role. As she gains a clearer understanding of how she and her children can respond to their change in life-style, she may feel ready again to consider a job change. On the other hand, she may elect to remain where she is for now, understanding that any more change may be an overload.

2. Should she elect to change jobs, Roberta seems to have a clear idea of what would be best for her own professional education. If she chooses to remain, however, she and her supervisor may need to address the following issues: Can her current position, possibly through assignment of additional special projects, be adapted to let her respond to interests in marketing, public relations, or fund raising? Is the student aid office in a position to consider its roles in fund raising or marketing? Is there a need for packaging student aid with financial planning? Here the strategy in forming a plan for Roberta's professional education would be to consider her additive stage of professional development: her desire to make a contribution to the institution as a whole and her special talents and interests.

Planning at the Institutional Level

Each chapter of this sourcebook makes the strong point that the professional education needs of staff vary according to individual development, educational mode, and proportion of contact with staff or students. The numerous means for providing professional education, as described in this sourcebook, suggest that the pathways to professional education provide interesting and satisfying journeys for those who use them. What seems to be missing is a systematic way of ensuring that all who wish to travel have road maps that lead to their chosen destinations.

As we examine existing delivery systems, we need first to consider variety in available alternatives. For example, a student affairs staff of sixty people at a hypothetical institution might typically include people who have been in their positions for fewer than two years; those whose time in their current positions ranges from three to five years; and others, who have held their current positions for more than five years. These same staff members may range in age from twenty-two to sixty-five. Many may have student personnel master's degrees, a few may have doctorates, some may have master's degrees in areas other than student affairs, and some may not have master's degrees.

To reach a staff with such diversity, our plans should include diverse modes of professional education: basic instruction; multiple opportunities to apply knowledge to the solution of real problems; and some opportunities to consider broader questions, such as the future role of student affairs at the institution, the effect of the knowledge explosion on higher education, and other such current issues. It should come as no surprise that this hypothetical institution's professional education committee would experience frustration in selecting a topic or topics to fit all these needs, deciding on a widely appealing presentation format, and even agreeing on the length of time to spend on the subjects selected.

An obvious solution might be to let each person do his or her own "thing," but cost, practicality, and the need to build staff morale and cohesion work against this option. At this point, the professional education committee may just pick a topic for the sake of getting anything at all planned, settle on a format that will at least hold the attention of most staff, and go about arranging the event, even with the lingering thought that something is missing.

That approach could be modified if the professional education committee presented two topics to the staff for consideration and asked them to choose one. After the topic was selected, each staff member might use the professional education model to assess his or her level of interest in the topic, prior knowledge in the area, preferred method of learning (or learning more) about the topic, and relevance of the topic to current position or future positions.

After this individual assessment, staff would be asked to submit concerns about the topic that reflected their own needs. The professional education committee might then plan a program to respond to those concerns. The program could be changed if staff were invited to attend certain activities, rather than attending the entire program. More time might be spent on the particular topic at each level of professional development (see the model in Chapter Two) and the format might move to a series of two-hour meetings spread over time. Individual staff with higher levels of knowledge might be used as presenters, and short audiotaped "lecturettes" might provide basic knowledge about the topic.

A second institutional alternative might be to select a year-long general theme for professional education. The theme could be related to the goals and objectives of the institution and of the student affairs area. Some examples of general themes are use of the CAS Standards as a planning document; understanding the political structures and norms of campus organizations; local research needs in student affairs; the role of student affairs staff in assessing and improving the quality of undergraduate instruction; performance evaluation of staff; the organization of campus student affairs functions and their relationship to institutional goals; coalition building and other methods of campuswide involvement in institutional issues; new approaches to delivering student services; future funding sources for higher education; and the role of student affairs staff in developing and using computer technology in student affairs.

An Example of Institutional Planning: Computer Technology. To accommodate the team-building/staff-cohesion needs of the institution, personnel from each functional area might meet with computer sales representatives and with staff members who are familiar with uses of computer technology in their areas. They could explore the benefits of using computer technology and generate some possible new programs—for example, damage billing with the housing office; a system of job and resumé banks in the placement office; course registration; room reservations via computer; monitoring of space utilization in the student union; and an accounting system for student activity budgets. Focusing attention on problems or needs together with people who know about computers offers an opportunity for staff to expand their own awareness of computer applications in their specialized areas. Once possibilities for computer uses are known, staff in each functional area might meet to discuss short- and long-range goals for computer use that are compatible with the mission and goals of both the institution and the student affairs division.

After these separate functional meetings, all the student affairs staff members could meet together to share the goals of their own areas and evaluate their compatibility with other areas and to identify common needs or times when cooperation between areas is needed. The entire staff would also be able to assess the extent of their current levels of knowledge about computers, to identify the knowledge levels needed to reach their goals, and to plan for adequate time to gain the computer knowledge they need. Staff who are already sophisticated with respect to computers might be identified as primary instructors for other staff (a role that could satisfy mentoring needs for some of them). Those who wish to take leadership roles in this professional education topic might prepare themselves by refreshing their own knowledge bases through attending a variety of regional and national convention programs on computers in higher education; visiting other colleges that have used computer technology in student affairs; and refreshing their teaching skills by arranging for one or more at-the-elbow experiences with those who have frequently instructed others about both basic knowledge and application of computer technology to current situations.

The staff members might agree that all of them, including clerical staff, must be computer literate, both in word-processing systems, and in administrative information systems. An each-one-teach-one model might pair clerical staff members with professional staff members, each having the opportunity to instruct the other in computer application. Staff who have similar types of contact with students and with staff might meet in workshops to focus on such topics as computers in direct service delivery to students; administrative information-management processes; implementation of new or improvement of existing applications of prepackaged software systems for information management; and equipment purchase and maintenance.

At the end of this year-long effort to provide education about the use of computer technology in many or all student affairs areas, the entire staff might come together once again to discuss broader issues reflective of knowledge update. These broader issues might include the balance between cost-effectiveness and the human factor in computer technology and direct student access to information systems related to academic advising, career planning, and job search. Finally, staff might use the following year to work toward goals in computer use, meeting again at the end of the second year to reassess staff and institutional needs for further professional education on this topic.

Summary

Professional education activities for student affairs staff should clearly benefit both individuals and institutions. When both sets of needs are taken into account in the planning of professional education activities, the "fit" between an institution and an individual staff member can only be enhanced. The professional education model allows individuals and entire staffs to plan systematically for professional education that will result in mutual gains. There is a sense of direction to professional education when an institution states its needs for competent staff members at all levels of interpersonal contact and when staff members recognize their own professional development stages and their own preferred modes of education in seeking that competence.

Staff members in this situation experience institutional support, in the form of time and money directed toward staff growth, and they understand more clearly the value of their contributions to the missions of their institutions. Institutions in this situation gain staff members whose increased competence is directly applied to institutional needs. It is still more cost-effective for an institution to provide professional education for current staff members than to hire new ones.

Leila V. Moore is currently director of Career Path Associates and assistant director for student organizations and program development at the Pennsylvania State University. She was formerly a professor of counseling and student personnel at the State University of New York at Albany, at the Pennsylvania State University, and at Bowling Green State University.

Graduate programs have been reluctant to meet the expanded educational needs of practitioners. As those needs increase, a solution will lie in the design of curricular offerings and instructional methodology that are both adaptable to practitioner needs and responsive to the needs of traditional graduate students.

Expanding Graduate Education

J. Roger Penn, Jo Anne J. Trow

In recent years, many fields have devoted increased attention to professional education. This trend is a direct result of the rapid changes occurring in our society: technological advancement, the information explosion, and shifting population patterns. As a society changes, so do the needs of its people. For professionals in many fields, including student affairs, the need to remain current, relevant, and actively involved is of paramount importance.

While some of this chapter stems from the literature about the professionalization of occupations, the primary focus here is on the need to expand professional education in student affairs, and on the role that graduate degree programs can play in this process. In our profession there appears to be a widening gap among theory, innovation, and practice. Graduate programs have been identified as a major resource in the effort to close this gap; however, the present structure of these programs provides little reason to believe that the gap will be closed in the near future.

Where We Are Now

Formal graduate education in student affairs began in the early 1900s. The first program was established by Esther Lloyd Jones at Colum-

L. V. Moore, R. B. Young (eds.). *Expanding Opportunities for Professional Education.*
New Directions for Student Services, no. 37. San Francisco: Jossey-Bass, Spring 1987.

bia University. The basis of this and other early programs was psychology and, as the field developed, counseling and mental health. Although programs in counseling produced student personnel practitioners in the pre–World War II years, it was not until the early 1950s that graduate programs were recognized to any extent. These programs, aside from Columbia University's, were oriented primarily toward the master's-level student seeking a counseling degree. Classroom learning was supplemented by internships in residence living and in a few other practicum settings. Up to the 1950s, many student affairs staff continued to come directly from academic teaching faculties or from other social service fields.

Within the last thirty years, however, graduate programs have multiplied across the country, so that many institutions now offer master's degrees and some even offer doctoral degrees in the field. Aside from presenting occasional programs at professional meetings or hosting regional workshops, faculty in these graduate programs have generally done little to respond to the professional education needs either of their graduates or of student affairs professionals already in the field. Rather, the purpose of these programs has been to provide the basic foundation and underpinning for the oftentimes young preprofessionals immediately out of undergraduate degree programs.

The idea that graduate programs should provide additional learning activities beyond the advanced-degree level has not received much credence either from professorial ranks in the programs or from professionals in the field. It is all too often noted that once a person leaves a graduate program, rarely is additional work pursued along traditional academic lines. The practitioner comes to believe that there is nothing to be gained from a return to the classroom and that the real learning is taking place in the world of action, which he or she experiences every day. With this focus on application, the practitioner pays little attention to the addition of new knowledge about the field. New ideas and approaches are discussed only at professional meetings and informal meetings with colleagues from other institutions or when there is a crisis (such as the current national and campus concern over drug and alcohol abuse). Many persons think that the inconvenience of taking more classes outweighs the importance of returning to campus to gain new knowledge and update skills.

Today we find that the curricula of most degree programs in student affairs are divided into three basic types (Delworth and Hanson, 1980). First, there are those with a counseling emphasis, in which students are trained in the theories and techniques of counseling and, through supervised internship experience, emerge prepared to work in settings that focus on one-to-one and group counseling.

Second, graduate programs with an administrative emphasis look more closely at the responsibilities and skills necessary to organize, complement, and coordinate programs and services in housing, student conduct, financial aid, student activities, placement, enrollment and records management, and general student affairs. Curricula focuses on organizational theory, developing management skills, understanding personnel issues, and working with budget and fiscal processes. Through practica, experience is frequently provided in a variety of specific offices and program areas.

The third and most recent type of curriculum emphasizes student development. Graduate programs with this thrust closely examine psychological development theories and adapt them to the world of post-secondary education. Classes focus on the process of working with students in different learning environments and helping students individually and in groups to determine their goals and implement them as part of the educational process.

Graduate programs, then, have sought to promote and teach a diverse set of theories and skills associated with counseling, administration, and student development. In terms of laying a foundation for entry into the field, the programs have been successful. An academic degree from one of these programs is almost a prerequisite for employment, regardless of the type of curricular offerings taken by the student. This is quite an accomplishment, considering that the field includes numerous subspecialties, and employs a wide range of staff with varied backgrounds. However, the question that must be asked is whether these programs can respond to the ongoing professional education needs of the student affairs professional who has completed at least one advanced degree. The adaptability of graduate programs to these new needs is questionable in light of the way most graduate programs are presently structured.

**Professional Education: Philosophical Foundations
and Assumptions**

More and more professional and lay members of our society have seen the need for lifelong learning in acquiring new knowledge and upgrading skills in order to meet the demands of today's workplace. In student affairs, some of the primary goals of lifelong learning are to provide opportunities for seasoned professionals to enhance their knowledge, improve their professional abilities, and adjust to the various role changes that are necessary for continued career success (Appleton, Briggs, and Rhatigan, 1978).

Learning, of course, can be accomplished in a number of ways. One can seek out knowledge and experience through self-instruction, interact on a one-to-one basis with mentors, or participate in formal courses, workshops, or seminars for academic credit. For professionals, end products can be improved knowledge, skills, and values and a permanent change in behavior, which brings about more effective practice or leads to career advancement.

From a philosophical point of view, the concept of professional education suggests that all individuals, especially adults, come to recognize which formal and informal experiences they need in order to be secure at different stages of their lives. Regardless of intelligence, age, or environmental setting, every person is capable of and in fact desires additional learning. For adults, the need for additional learning is stimulated by factors related to interpersonal, social, and career roles and expectations. Ongoing education can be proposed as a major contributor to professional self-worth and productivity (Merriam, 1977).

As Young notes in Chapter Two, for professionals in the field of student affairs, each stage of career or professional development brings recognition of new goals and unique needs associated with remaining an effective practitioner. To respond to these goals and needs, individuals, regardless of career stage, must identify means to improve knowledge and skills within their own limitations of time and place. The ultimate concern is to release human potential and control the conditions of one's professional and personal life by maintaining a sense of competence and worthiness (Knowles, 1980). Failure to do so can often result in a sense of helplessness, rejection, loss of control, lack of self-esteem, and "burnout." Thus, the primary philosophical basis of ongoing professional education is that education should be related to current life circumstances and should focus on the learner's active participation and on the development of educational opportunities and activities.

At the same time, ongoing professional education conceptualizes the learner and the learning relationship in a particular manner, with assumptions about the process of learning (Darkenwald and Merriam, 1982). In general, it is held that motivation for learning essentially evolves from one's need to interact effectively with and control various aspects of one's life. The need for learning, therefore, is lifelong and is connected to each stage of development. Each stage is a response to the previous stage. As one grows older and matures, each stage becomes integrated with the previous stage. Therefore, effective methods and activities of learning (or "modes of education," as discussed by Young in Chapter Two) are responsive to the current stage of career or professional development and to the professional role. Learning opportunities, then, should be available and structured so as to permit easy access through a variety of settings. They should be obtainable in a timely fashion, involve the learner in the design process, and be responsive to current needs.

Assessing and Responding to Staff Needs

The need for professional education in our field can be richly illustrated. It is important and significant to people who are making transitions from one professional development stage to another, who desire to do "something different," who are assigned new responsibilities, or who are satisfied with their present responsibilities and seek to refine their skills. Yet, to be effective and to have the maximum impact on the individual, as well as on the organization, a number of practical considerations need to be taken into account, and some organizational constraints must be overcome. In many ways, these challenges are very similar to those associated with the success or failure of professional education activities in the field (Delworth, 1978; Beeler and Penn, 1979).

To those who have studied the origins and evolution of our field, these challenges come as no surprise. As Brown notes in Chapter One, student affairs has often been characterized as a somewhat poorly defined enterprise, which is based on a number of academic disciplines, marked by a wide range of loosely associated activities, and staffed by professionals from diverse backgrounds and with varied educational preparation. Individuals within the field also work in a wide range of different types of institutions of postsecondary education, each requiring a somewhat different approach to the delivery of programs and services. The field itself is as diverse as the professionals who work in it—counselors, deans of students, financial aid administrators, directors of student housing, admissions officers, college union directors, student activities coordinators, and other staff responsible for related programs (Packwood, 1977). Here, we find a broad range of backgrounds, differing areas of specialization, and varying levels of expertise. While all these staff need professional education, the needs of staff members who work primarily with students differ from those of staff members who work with students and staff; and both kinds of needs differ dramatically from those of persons who work almost exclusively with staff. It is not a matter of preparing for a position in student affairs but rather of preparing to be adaptable and flexible and of remaining effective over one's entire career (Shaffer, 1984). As Tilley (1973) has noted, staff working in the field of student affairs "can be characterized as professionals in the process of becoming" (p. 119).

Because of the multiple requirements of the average staff member's job and the wide range of backgrounds and levels of expertise that exist within the field, it is not surprising that to provide professional education to meet all needs is generally viewed as impossible. The primary goal of professional education must be to improve the performance of staff in their present roles while providing a climate in which personal and professional growth can occur in the best interests of individuals, institutions, and the profession.

Preparing the Way for Professional Education

Concern has been expressed in recent years that graduate programs in student affairs may not be responding to the needs of the broad array of professionals currently on the job and working in the field (Garland, 1985; Young, 1985). Little wonder, in view of the set of circumstances described here, that professional education is given only lip service in many colleges and universities; yet we know that opportunities for formal and informal education enhance and contribute directly to personal and professional survival in this era of rapid change.

As we approach the 1990s, higher education is wracked by controversy, frustration, and retrenchment. A primary concern during this period will be institutional renewal. How will institutions of higher learning bring about creative change and remain dynamic, given the constraints they face? As priorities are reordered, and as "steady-state" becomes the way of the future, it will be essential to discover new and better ways to meet contemporary needs. A crucial element of this process, especially in our field, will be the continual development of staff, and graduate programs can be in a position to make significant contributions if they restructure themselves to be responsive to the professional education needs of new as well as seasoned staff (Brown, 1985).

For new professionals, or for individuals in student-centered positions, education received through graduate programs is largely sufficient to meet on-the-job needs, and this is as it should be. For other staff members, however, that foundation already exists and the conveying of basic information through coursework may not be as essential as other modes of learning, as Young notes in Chapter Two.

This fact is frequently acknowledged both by faculty and by students in graduate programs. Among staff who are beyond the early stages of their careers and who have entered graduate programs, it is not uncommon to hear such comments as "Instructors may know the principles but don't have insight into how to apply them" or "The instructor's ideas are good in theory but will never work in practice." Faculty who are sensitive to this issue are equally frustrated because, in reality, traditional instructional techniques do limit the ability to apply theory effectively.

In general, graduate programs use the same techniques of instruction that are designed for undergraduate students. These techniques focus on the mastery of facts and information as well as on the ability of students to recall facts and information. With the exception of thesis-writing assignments, the process largely excludes student involvement and can foster passive attitudes toward learning. The limitations of the traditional teaching process are especially evident when students are middle- and senior-level staff with at least one advanced degree and when they have played active and responsible roles in their professions, families, and communities.

Educational theory holds that adults learn better when they take the initiative and the responsibility for learning, rather than relying on the traditional teacher-student relationship (Harrington, 1977). Graduate faculty should give thorough consideration to expanding their instructional techniques, becoming familiar with adult-learning theory, and applying appropriate methods to the educational needs of people advanced beyond the early years of professional development. Faculty need to understand that most adult learners at the graduate level are highly self-directed and have clearly defined educational goals. The key is to structure graduate programs and their related educational and learning resources so that they are easily accessible and respond adequately to learner's needs. How can this be accomplished?

First, and probably most important, faculty in graduate programs should undertake review and throrough diagnosis of their course offerings (Brown, 1985), as well as of their methods and means of instructional delivery. Next, learners, in consultation with faculty, need to undertake professional education assessments, perhaps by means of the process described by Moore in Chapter Three. These steps should result in clarification of programs' missions and goals, in addition to development of strategies for meeting the needs of adult learners. Graduate faculty have the responsibility of providing a variety of learning avenues by which educational goals can be accomplished. Students and faculty need to participate jointly in the planning of educational experiences, to communicate actively throughout, and to share in the evaluation of experiences in light of developmental levels of staff members.

The success or failure of such an approach depends on graduate faculty members' taking the lead in altering traditional structures. It should be remembered that university and departmental requirements do offer great flexibility in structuring program goals, course content, and instructional methodologies. Instructors have a high degree of freedom in how they approach the learning process. Success will also be determined by the willingness of faculty as a whole to be committed to an instructional model that recognizes the needs of student affairs staff as unique adult learners.

The instruction must differ from common, traditional approaches (van Aalst, 1979). Probably the best strategy is to award credit for a combination of formal coursework, attendance at workshops, participation in conferences and seminars, independent study, and experiential learning. In this way, the learner can draw on a variety of resources, including the formal classroom, the job environment, the library, and the field experience. While experienced staff may be secure and confident in their abilities on the job, as students they may face high uncertainty about their academic abilities. The focus needs to be on what is learned and on how it applies to being a professional in the field, rather than on compliance with a structured experience whose culmination is a grade and eventually a degree.

By taking factors such as these into consideration, graduate programs will be far more able to respond to ongoing professional education

46

needs. In addition, program faculty will need to add new instructional techniques and modify current approaches.

New Modified Instructional Techniques

Creating a learning environment that is sensitive to adult learners is a major challenge. However, the philosophy of professional education suggests that adult learners are aware of their educational needs, able to identify specific goals in response to these needs, committed to achieving these goals when intimately involved in designing learning programs, and able to evaluate their own performance. There follows a list of instructional methodologies that might be considered for adoption and implementation.

Faculty as Tutors. This approach suggests a more intensive relationship between the instructor and the learner than is usually found in graduate programs. Here, the primary role of the instructor is to provide a foundation for learning and then to challenge the learner through questioning and probing, as well as to analyze and evaluate the learner's responses. In this sense, learning becomes a communal activity, in which instructors and students, through frequent interaction, come to consensus on learning goals, methods, and evaluation criteria. Faculty function as tutors rather than as transmitters of information. The goal is to enhance in-depth learning.

Learning Contracts. One practical approach frequently used in professional education programs entails the use of "learning contracts," which systematize the teacher-learner relationship. The central elements include identification of learners' goals, assessment of learner's strengths and weaknesses, and negotiation with instructors on activities for achieving professional growth through education. The willingness of the learner to be candid is of paramount importance, like the role of the instructor as teacher and advisor for assessment purposes. The end product is a written document, which outlines the details of a professional education plan.

Case Studies. In order to permit learners to relate on-the-job performance learning to curriculum learning, the case-study approach can be a valuable instructional technique. When students and instructors collaborate in presenting and discussing actual cases, a sound climate for practical learning is established. Although cases are often used, along with other approaches in some courses, the case study should be routinely used as a technique for integrating out-of-class and in-class learning. Experienced, current practitioners can join graduate faculty in a team-teaching format, creating a bridge between the requirements of the formal curriculum and the learner's actual work experience and professional education goals. Both student and instructor learn.

Resource Centers. In addition to the formal curricula offered in graduate programs, planners should consider creating learning and resource centers to focus on the needs of experienced staff. Centers of this kind could provide all the essential resources that are needed for self-evaluation and self-study. The task for faculty and students would be to identify and analyze professional education goals and to amass the resources that would permit students to acquire the skills needed to achieve the goals. (The professional education center described in Chapter Five might meet many of these needs.)

Consortium Relationships. Another plan would be for graduate programs to take the lead in developing and entering into consortium relationships with the divisions of student affairs at the many colleges and universities that do not have formal, graduate offerings. Workshops, seminars, and instructor-student interaction would be provided for the purpose of responding to professional education needs of staff who are not necessarily interested in seeking advanced degrees. By means of sharing resources in the consortium, other on-campus educational activities could be regularly provided.

Mentoring. Mentoring, as it relates to the professional education of student affairs staff, is often overlooked. As defined by Moore (1982), mentoring is a form of adult socialization for professional roles, especially leadership roles. Faculty in graduate education can assist this process in two ways. First, they themselves can be mentors for young professionals, helping those new to the field to make contacts and find appropriate employment. More important, however, instructors can identify promising leaders for the profession and encourage these potential leaders to accept responsibility, take risks, and take advantage of varied professional opportunities. Second, faculty should understand both the importance of mentoring and the impact it can have on the performance and subsequent commitment of all professionals in the field. By playing the role of mentor over the years, faculty can renew and strengthen the professional commitment of their former students and current associates. In other words, graduate education should not stop with the awarding of the degree but should flourish in subsequent years through continued contact and ongoing communication.

Faculty Fellowships and Exchanges. Most colleges and universities do not have graduate programs in student affairs administration. Thus (even for staff at institutions with graduate programs who do not wish to take courses at those institutions) the creation of faculty fellowships and staff exchanges provides an attractive opportunity for professional education. Chief student affairs officers, department heads, or staff education committees should promote exchanges or consider developing faculty fellowships in professional education for a term or even for an academic year. Using this approach, staff at a given institution would identify high-priority professional education needs and then acquire the services of graduate faculty members to develop and coordinate appropriate learning experiences that respond to these needs. Most graduate faculty members would welcome the opportunity to be in residence at different institutions for a time and would also benefit from the experience themselves. Moreover, graduate programs often need a "shot in the arm," easily obtained through an exchange. A program could acquire the instructional services of a seasoned practitioner, who would welcome the opportunity to receive a courtesy faculty appointment and who would provide both formal and informal learning opportunities to graduate students and to practitioners. With this approach, the possibilities are nearly unlimited for the professional education of all parties concerned.

Institutes. On occasion, professional associations sponsor institutes to consider topics of importance to practitioners. The role graduate programs can play in this process, however, is often overlooked. Graduate faculty are often on the leading edge of emerging issues, trends, and theory, and much of this information is best presented in seminars or symposia. Graduate programs, institutions without graduate programs, and professional associations should seek each other out and join as partners in the delivery of relevant professional education.

The Challenge for Graduate Programs

It is interesting to note that in the last two decades many colleges and universities have become institutions designed predominantly to serve adult undergraduate as well as graduate learners. While this fact is well known among those in student affairs, our own graduate programs seem disappointingly and minimally responsive to the educational needs of staff already in the field.

Besides offering advanced degrees, graduate programs should explore new and expanded ways of providing professional education. The structure of most programs, however, seems to deter their use for non-degree professional education. Likewise, graduate faculty may feel uneasy when confronted with the questions and comments of practitioners who have extensive experience in the field and who want to upgrade their knowledge and skills. Because of their own lack of current administrative experience, faculty may also feel frustrated in their attempts to close the gap between theory and practice. Furthermore, institutional constraints, such as teaching and advising loads, may prevent graduate faculty from attending to their own professional education needs and serving others better.

If the concept of professional education is to be adopted and formally recognized by our profession, then graduate faculty, as well as practitioners in the field, must recognize the continuing importance of professional education. Supervisors of student affairs divisions must understand the personal and organizational benefits of retaining competent staff members and must encourage increased access to professional education opportunities. Graduate programs must offer a wide range of instructional approaches, formal and informal, as well as curricular offerings. Supervisors must promote the development of initiative and risk taking by staff members. Instructors will need to shift their attention away from texts and lectures (and, indeed, sometimes away from themselves). Learners will need to maintain a sense of curiosity, to be assertive, and to commit themselves to the concept of professional education throughout their professional lifetimes. Change is the only constant that we in student affairs can count on, and individual staff members must be prepared to cope with it. These recommendations, if followed, will do much to promote a climate conducive to professional education in our field.

Summary

The primary purpose of graduate programs in our field has been to prepare competent practitioners for specific jobs in colleges and universities. Because of a combination of historical tradition and circumstance, graduate programs have often been criticized for being unresponsive to the needs of practitioners. There is frequently a rift between those who teach in graduate programs and those who practice. Faculty and practitioners alike need to critique and evaluate the relevance and appropriateness of curricula, as well as the means by which curricula are delivered. The instructional techniques suggested in this chapter could easily be adapted to graduate programs whose planners wish to be more responsive to the needs and interests of experienced staff. For new or entry-level staff members, perhaps the most important things graduate programs can do are to set the stage for professionalism and to create a desire for professional education and lifelong learning, regardless of the individual's present career stage.

Realistically, any effort to expand professional education represents a cost to the college or university, as well as to the individual. However, the benefits that result far outweigh the costs. A commitment to the concept of professional education should be viewed as an investment in the future. For the individual, professional education provides opportunities for increasing knowledge, improving skills or gaining new ones, and qualifying for promotion or other job changes. For the institution, the benefits include a clear understanding of performance standards, greater flexibility in responding to staffing needs, a more stable work force, increased group morale, and improved efficiency. Reduction in staff dissatisfaction, improved overall productivity, increased commitment to the job, and greater loyalty to the organization can be expected.

The need for highly qualified and competent professional staff members in student affairs has never been greater, for several obvious reasons. Today many institutions of higher learning, faced with financial exigencies, have called for accountability from programs and personnel alike. The profession of student affairs is asked to justify its contributions and its staff positions. High staff turnover is a thing of the past; a constant influx of new staff members can no longer be counted on as a primary source of valuable ideas and fresh insights into emerging issues and trends. Instead, institutions must look for cost-effective methods of retraining and diversifying current staff so as to ensure their own adaptation to changes in higher education. The challenge of the future will be for graduate faculty and practitioners on the job to join in making professional education adaptive to the shifting needs of higher education and readily available as a central element of the professionalization of the field. As Shaffer stressed (1979, p. 1), "Some skills and approaches will always be in order. However, many others must be adopted . . . and new procedures implemented based on current concepts and technology. Questions arise . . . who will introduce the new . . . [and] who will lead the way . . . ?"

References

Appleton, J., Briggs, C., and Rhatigan, J. (eds.). *Pieces of Eight: The Rights, Roles, and Styles of the Dean by Eight Who Have Been There.* Portland: National Institute of Research and Development of NASPA, 1978.

Beeler, K., and Penn, J. R. *A Handbook on Staff Development in Student Affairs.* Corvallis: Oregon State University, 1979.

Brown, R. "Graduate Education for the Student Development Educator: A Content and Process Model." *NASPA Journal,* 1985, *22,* 39–43.

Darkenwald, G., and Merriam, S. *Adult Education: Foundations of Practice.* New York: Harper & Row, 1982.

Delworth, U. (ed.). *Training Competent Staff.* New Directions for Student Services, no. 2. San Francisco: Jossey-Bass, 1978.

Delworth, U., Hanson, G. R., and Associates. *Student Services: A Handbook for the Profession.* San Francisco: Jossey-Bass, 1980.

Garland, P. *Serving More Than Students: A Critical Need for College Student Personnel Services.* AAHE-ERIC Higher Education Research Report no. 7. Washington: American Association of Higher Education, 1985.

Harrington, F. H. *The Future of Adult Education: New Responsibilities of Colleges and Universities.* San Francisco: Jossey-Bass, 1977.

Knowles, M. *The Modern Practice of Adult Education.* Chicago: Follett, 1980.

Merriam, S. "Philosophical Perspectives on Adult Education: A Critical Review of the Literature." *Adult Education,* 1977, *27,* 195–208.

Moore, K. *What To Do Until the Mentor Arrives.* Washington, D.C.: National Association of Women Administrators, Deans and Counselors, 1982.

Packwood, W. (ed.). *College Student Personnel Services.* Springfield: Thomas, 1977.

Shaffer, R. "Introduction." In J. R. Penn and K. Beeler (eds.), *A Handbook on Staff Development in Student Affairs.* Corvallis: Oregon State University, 1979.

Shaffer, R. "Preparing for Student Personnel in the 1980s." In A. Kirby and D. Woodward (eds.), *Career Perspectives in Student Affairs.* Columbus, Ohio: National Association of Student Personnel Administrators, 1984.

Tilley, D. "Student Services and the Politics of Survival." In J. Katz (ed.), *Services for Students*. New Directions for Higher Education, no. 3. San Francisco: Jossey-Bass, 1973.

van Aalst, F. D. (ed.). *Combining Career Development with Experiential Learning*. New Directions for Experiential Learning, no. 5. San Francisco: Jossey-Bass, 1979.

Young, R. "Impressions of the Development of Professional Identity: From Program to Practice." *NASPA Journal*, 1985, *23*, 50–60.

J. Roger Penn is assistant vice-president for student affairs, professor of education, and director of the college student services administration graduate program at Oregon State University.

Jo Anne J. Trow is vice-president for student affairs and professor of education at Oregon State University.

*Institutions should promote these alternatives for expanding
professional education for student affairs practitioners: in-
service programs, professional exchanges, and regional
professional education centers.*

Institutional Alternatives
for Expanding
Professional Education

*Thomas D. Aceto, William A. Bryan,
Robert B. Young*

This chapter introduces three institutional alternatives for the professional
education of student affairs staff. Institutional in-service is described in the
first section with information from an informal national survey of offerings. The second section discusses professional exchanges for student
affairs administrators and counselors. The third section describes an effort
to establish a professional development center for graduate students and
practitioners in New York and New England. The chapter concludes with
a brief description of the ways in which these alternatives relate to the
model of professional education.

Institutional In-Service

One's education as a professional does not cease with the completion of a graduate program of study, even at the doctoral level. The acqui-
sition of new knowledge, the mastery of new skills, and the refinement of
earlier-acquired skills are important elements in an institutional program

L. V. Moore, R. B. Young (eds.). *Expanding Opportunities for Professional Education.*
New Directions for Student Services, no. 37. San Francisco: Jossey-Bass, Spring 1987.

of professional education for student affairs staff. While specific elements of staff development may vary—to reflect the type and size of an institution, the professional developmental stages of individual staff members, and the variety of tasks to be performed—there are some broad purposes, thematic content areas, and approaches common to most institutionally based programs.

In establishing institutional programs of professional education, it is necessary to consider the different educational needs of staff members, as reflected in staff's ages and career stages, the ratio of their interactions with other staff and with students, the modes of education in which they are engaged, and their own career aspirations. A thorough understanding of these educational needs is necessary before goals, objectives, strategies, and assessment of an in-service effort can be intelligently pursued.

Beginning a Program. A program usually evolves from the work of a departmental or divisional staff education committee. The committee deserves broad representation among the staff, including people in all modes of education, with all ratios of staff-student interaction, and at all professional development stages. This committee identifies the educational needs and interests of staff. It seeks information on what should be learned and how it might be learned. The objectivity and thoroughness of this assessment are essential, while the format is less so. It might be accomplished by a questionnaire, individual interviews, group brainstorming, or some other techniques. (Moore, in Chapter Three, has suggested an interview protocol for accomplishing this assessment.) While individual staff members are probably in the best position to identify their own professional education needs, their immediate supervisors should not be overlooked as sources of valid observations and suggestions on content areas and processes of learning.

The importance of the staff education committee cannot be overstated. Too often, programs are haphazardly created because of insufficient charge to and constituency of this committee. Membership frequently falls to the newest and least experienced staff members. Speakers and topics are chosen by dominant members. Opinions are not tempered by objective assessments. Committees do not receive the necessary status and recognition from the chief student affairs officer or from the president. They do not have the time or the breadth and continuity of membership to develop long-range assessments, policies, and programs for professional education.

Assumptions and Purposes. Professional education is based on certain unstated assumptions. Foremost is the premise that student affairs professionals should be actively involved in their own development, in order to meet the developmental needs of students and subordinate staff. Because of this, professionals in student affairs are assumed to be motivated toward continual growth and improvement in their professional practice. While individuals are ultimately responsible for their own professional education, the organization must accept some responsibility for providing opportunities and stimulation. However, the organization should not accept a strategy of maintenance (that is, static development) vis-à-vis its activities or those of its staff; rather, it should have a strategy of planned improvement.

Beginning with these assumptions, and using information gathered through the assessment of staff needs and interests, one should prepare a statement of purpose for professional education, a statement that can provide meaning and direction to the staff education committee. This statement is often presented in terms of some specific goal to be attained: to promote personal and career growth; to encourage staff to acquire and refine professional skills, abilities, and attitudes; to help staff to explore and build their commitment to the profession; to promote commitment to the mission of the institution; or to enhance organizational vitality.

Structural Levels of Institutional Programs. Professional education occurs at many levels within an institution. It may involve a prescribed set of activities designed for a single staff member, or an institutionwide workshop addressing a need common to all professional staff. It may involve a sabbatical leave, an exchange arrangement between staff members at different institutions, or a workshop aimed at the members of a single department. While the alternatives are many and diverse, most activities can be assigned to one of four kinds of programs: institutional, divisional, departmental, or individual.

Most in-service training provides a variety of activities and opportunities across all four of these categories. Typically, institutionwide programs are generated by offices of personnel services or employee relations or, in the case of statewide systems of higher education, by system offices. The formats tend to use large-group lectures, workshops, or seminars, and topics tend to be generic ("Effective Office Management," "Personal Financial Planning," "Basic Supervision," "Introduction to the Microcomputer"). When such programs meet the needs and interests of student affairs practitioners, they do not have to be offered at the divisional or departmental levels. However, specific educational needs of student affairs practitioners can best be addressed at the divisional, departmental, and individual program levels.

Divisional programs employ a variety of format and topics. It is not unusual to find general staff meetings, retreats, summer conferences, brown-bag seminars, newsletters, workshops, and other mechanisms designed to bring professionals together for a shared learning experience. Several factors will influence the choice of a presentation format. Among the more important are the target audience, the intent of the activity, and the delivery of the activity.

At the divisional level, topics tend to be generic to the student affairs profession or to the nature of student affairs operations. Current topics include computer uses, stress management, wellness, alcohol control, time management, teamwork and communication, liability, the Myers-Briggs Type Indicator, and conflict resolution.

In addition to group activities, divisional staff education can include other efforts. A divisional resource library might be established, to include professional books, journals, audiotapes and videotapes, other professional materials, a copy machine, a word processor, and lists of what else is available in departmental libraries. Another activity might entail the distribution of a conference and workshop summary form, to be completed by all staff who attend such meetings. A third effort might be to publish a divisional newsletter covering professional issues on the local, regional, and national levels.

Departmental programs tend to focus on specific professional practices. In contrast with divisional programs, professional education activities are offered on a more regular, routine basis and are often linked with weekly staff meetings. Workshops, retreats, featured speakers, case studies, and brown-bag lunches on selected issues represent the usual format for departmental in-service education. As one would expect, topics vary by department.

Departmental programs can address the personal-growth needs and interests of staff. Physical wellness, personal finance, personal liability, and stress management are topics likely to appear on departmental in-service program calendars. The relationship between personal growth and professional performance demands attention at the departmental level. Thus, some of the most intense professional education will occur at this level in the in-service program.

Professional education should be personalized to whatever possible extent, and use of the professional education model supplies ways to personalize education. With respect to modes of education, staff can be offered opportunities to enroll in courses, attend conferences and workshops, serve as interns, receive released time to engage in research or other scholarly activity, or negotiate "growth contracts." These options should supplement what is available through any additional institutionwide, divisional, and departmental programs. These options enable institutions to respond to unique or unusual needs that cannot be satisfied through group mechanisms.

Professional Exchanges

Budget restrictions have limited the mobility of many faculty and staff in higher education. They have challenged colleges, universities, and professional associations to create new educational options for professional staff. One important option is the professional exchange of staff between campuses. Professional exchanges diminish staff burnout and job frustration by offering a change in work environment and responsibilities. In addition, exchanges enable staff to attend to their own professional development by establishing mentor relationships outside their own institutions.

Professional exchanges can be developed at campus, state, regional, or national levels. Most of this discussion concerns campus-level efforts, but a state or regional professional exchange center can be established by institutions working together, perhaps within a framework that has been developed by professional associations. Private institutions might be involved in such centers, since they can have greater flexibility in establishing exchanges. Public colleges and universities must deal with state regulations regarding pay, travel, supervisory arrangements, and duration of professional leave. Such regulations impede the development of exchanges.

The most prominent professional exchange center is the National Faculty Exchange (National Faculty Exchange, 1984–85), funded by the Exxon Education Foundation, the Ford Foundation, and institutional membership fees. The National Faculty Exchange is in its fifth year of operation. It offers exchange opportunities for faculty and staff in colleges and universities throughout the United States.

Guidelines for a student affairs professional exchange center need to be established at the outset. They should account for the special interest of employees, of home institutions, and of host institutions. The responsibilities of the employees and institutions must be explicit so that the exchange program can accomplish its goals with a minimum of administrative confusion.

These guidelines should be developed through face-to-face negotiations. Individuals from the home and host institutions must meet and agree on professional education goals, such as offering opportunities for staff who wish to pursue advanced degrees, facilitating the efforts of staff who want to examine different career responsibilities, and building new skills among staff. The negotiations are intricate, and detail is important; advantages for professional staff must outweigh potential problems.

The chief student affairs officer must support professional exchanges in order for them to succeed. He or she controls the remuneration, job responsibilities, and professional leave of staff who might participate in an exchange. That determines the extent of staff participation and thus the fate of the program.

The effectiveness of a professional exchange program may be based on (1) the accomplishment of goals that are identified by staff desiring to exchange campuses; (2) an assessment of any limitations of the exchange setting, and on the receptivity of the host campus to the person who is a guest; (3) a formalized, participant-led review process for feedback and improvement; (4) a review of the performance of staff members once they return to their home campuses; and (5) the willingness of campuses and

58

individuals to risk temporarily and possibly sacrifice the depth of some service(s) in order to provide the opportunity for staff to gain new knowledge and new experiences.

Professional exchanges offer advantages to campus management and participating staff. The advantages to management include renewed vitality among staff and the infusion of new ideas into the home and host campuses. Participating staff are able to get and give expertise in new settings. They can pursue particular interests, which will increase their effectiveness when they return to their home campuses. They develop reciprocal relationships, which can be maintained after the exchange. Participating staff can renew their energy and sharpen their skills; they can regain the full use of their "human capital" on the modern-day campus.

Professional Education Centers

While other sections of this chapter have offered guidelines, for the establishment of in-service programs and professional exchanges, this section describes a specific effort to establish a professional education center, thus presenting general guidelines for establishing future centers.

In 1983, the graduate faculty at the University of Vermont attempted to create a center for professional education in student affairs in Bennington, Vermont. The project was guided by the recommendations of the American College Personnel Association (ACPA) planning document, *Action Planning for the Eighties* (Bloland and others, 1982). The document stated that graduate preparation programs should provide outreach education in order to diffuse theory and related practice in professional education. Because of its proximity to several population centers, the planners thought that a facility in Bennington could serve the professional education needs of eastern New York and most of New England.

A needs assessment of the student affairs staffs at the colleges and universities within a one-hour driving radius of Bennington revealed sufficient support for the center. A program of seminars was developed as a pilot test to determine whether staff and graduate students would actually travel to Bennington for professional education. The program was publicized widely in the region, and by the time the third seminar was held, enrollments indicated a strong need for professional education in the area.

As the professional education needs emerged, three types of programs seemed appropriate: off-campus masters' degree programs; post-master's certificate programs in adult development, counseling, and student affairs administration; and one-day professional education seminars on various topics in higher education. The programs were designed to attract two different populations of learners: people with baccalaureate degrees who were employed in student affairs or aspiring to that employment, and people with advanced degrees who wanted to improve their professional skills.

There were also a timetable for development and a budget. The timetable indicated that a permanent center could be established in Bennington by September 1984. That goal involved the establishment of a professional education office in Bennington; the confirmation of seminars and courses; grant applications; marketing; the completion of paperwork for degree programs; and the development of research projects. The budget proposal requested a three-quarter-time administrator and a secretary, with the administrator to receive additional revenue from course instruction.

All the services of the center were designed to provide maximum accessibility for the participants. Nontraditional scheduling and teaching would be the rule. Long-range plans included the development of videotapes and learning packages for rent; conference-call seminars; grants for center programs and staff; internships for graduate students at designated sites; consortia; and professional exchanges of administrators through Bennington. The center would promote the ACPA Generativity and Professional Exchange Center Projects as well.

In the end, the center was not established, despite its potential. However, experience in developing plans for the center yielded several positive outcomes. It provided knowledge about in-service education in student affairs, which benefited national, regional, and state professional associations. Planning for the center also affirmed that preparation and professional education did not have to be mutually exclusive; their interaction could yield practical benefits both for graduate programs and for current practitioners. It was also shown that the center could have produced a profit for the sponsoring graduate preparation program.

Student affairs needs to develop professional education centers, such as the center described here, to provide opportunities for innovative instruction (which Penn and Trow note in Chapter Four). Graduate students and student affairs practitioners need to interact, to test the boundaries of theory and practice, and to integrate theory with practice for the betterment of higher education.

Relation of the Alternatives to the Professional Education Model Presented in Chapter Two

This chapter describes three ways in which institutions can expand professional education for student affairs practitioners. These alternatives address the needs of practitioners in different stages of education through the use of different modes of delivery. A professional education center promotes the interaction of professionals across the gamut of career stages: formative, application, and additive. Institutional in-service programs meet the needs of application and additive professionals, while professional exchanges usually boost application professionals toward the additive stage.

The alternatives emphasize different modes of professional education. Institutional in-service is based on performance learning, even relating per-

60

sonal dimensions of growth to performance. When professional exchanges are implemented as extensions of institutional in-service programs, they also involve performance learning. Professional education centers facilitate inquiry learning among senior professionals, but their hallmark might be the ability to relate instruction to performance needs. Full-time practitioners can show full-time graduate students the ways in which their classroom experiences relate (or don't relate) to on-the-job needs.

None of the alternatives present in this chapter isolates the dimension of interpersonal contact. Institutional in-service, professional exchanges, and regional education centers also can rejuvenate counselors and administrators.

Professional exchanges and regional education centers have not been implemented in student affairs, despite their apparent potential. This might be true, in part, because no one has explained their uniqueness in terms of the model of professional education. Foundations might grant funds for exchanges and development centers if they could be convinced of the uniqueness of merit of these alternatives. As well, institutions have not tried to create exchanges or professional education centers because of the legal and technical problems involved. It is easier to let other colleges and universities create these facilities and then copy them or utilize them as consumers. But, while some institutions wait for others to do the groundwork, the student affairs staffs of all institutions are growing more dependent on improved professional education. Ultimately, initial technical difficulties are easier to overcome than the incompetence of staff. Professional exchanges and education centers do not have to be initiated on a grand scale. Little implementations can make a big difference in the future of professional education in student affairs.

References

Bloland, P., Blaesser, W., Butler, W., Lewis, C., and Shaffer, R. *Action Planning for the Eighties.* Falls Church, Va.: American College Personnel Association, 1982.
National Faculty Exchange. *National Faculty Exchange Annual Report.* Fort Wayne, Ind.: National Faculty Exchange, 1984–85.

Thomas D. Aceto is vice-president for student and administrative services at the University of Maine.

William A. Bryan is vice-chancellor for student affairs at the University of North Carolina, Wilmington.

Robert B. Young is associate professor and program adviser for higher education administration and coordinator of faculty development for the College of Education at Kent State University.

*The role of state, regional, and national associations in the
professional education of student affairs administrators
and counselors is investigated.*

The Role of Professional Associations

Marian Schrank, Robert B. Young

This chapter discusses the professional education activities of state,
regional, and national associations. Associations determine the educational
standards of professions. Their conferences are important educational experiences. It is not uncommon for the members of a profession to affiliate
with organizations with which they share a commonality of goals and
purposes. The need to collectively express views and opinions is evident
in the success of these organizations, which have attracted the membership
of nearly half of the twenty million managerial and professional workers
in the United States (Healy, 1982).

State Associations

The member/association relationship should be a mutual partnership. Members want to know what the association can offer them and
what their role will be in return. A mutual partnership is usually found
in the membership of statewide or regional associations.

The strength of state associations lies in their grass-roots foundation. As feeder networks to national organizations, state groups can attend
to the professional education of student affairs staff at the local level.
Utilizing their greater resources, state associations can go beyond the pro-

L. V. Moore, R. B. Young (eds.). *Expanding Opportunities for Professional Education.*
New Directions for Student Services, no. 37. San Francisco: Jossey-Bass, Spring 1987.

fessional education available within an institution and yet operate within a framework that is also responsive to particular campus needs. The union among members is enhanced by the comfortable, close-knit environment of the state setting, which can draw on similar regional issues while it acknowledges a diversity of confidence and competence.

State associations share the broad purposes of national associations. State associations also showcase institutional programs, procedures, and activities, thus furthering knowledge about the field. They identify local leadership within the profession. They explore institutional solutions to regional problems before they become crises. State associations keep practitioners abreast of regional concerns. They create networks of professionals and institutions within a region.

Recently, the College Student Personnel Association of New York State (Schoonmaker, 1985) conducted an evaluation and planning survey. Over 600 members were asked about the relevance and effectiveness of the organization. The members affirmed that their professional education needs were being met by this statewide association. Of greatest value were networking, camaraderie, professionalism of the leadership, quality of the conferences, grass-roots philosophy of the organization, opportunity for participation, exchange of information, and commitment by the organization to quality in higher education.

Regional Associations

Regional associations are situated between state and national associations. They articulate the needs of both the others, yet they offer a different scope of activities. The regional association can be a subunit of a national organization, such as the regional groups of the National Association of Student Personnel Administrators (NASPA). It might also be an informal grouping of state associations that join together for a specific purpose, for example, the New England state associations of the American College Personnel Association (ACPA) coordinated a regional conference in 1984.

Strengths of Regional Associations. Four strengths typify regional associations: they bring together diverse people within a region; they serve groups that have no other organization; they deal with regional issues more effectively than state or national associations; and they consolidate resources for improved educational conferences.

Regional activities bring together diverse people. Although the National Association of College Activities (NACA) and the Association of College Unions-International (ACU-I) deal with the functional area of student activities, their members often differ in age and professional experience. At the annual joint national conference of both associations, the undergraduate student representatives of NACA are separated from the senior administrators of ACU-I. Within any state, there may be neither enough members nor enough resources for a professional education conference of either association to function. However, at regional conferences, the young affiliates of NACA can interact with the professional affiliates of ACU-I, identifying their separate needs and sharing mutual interests.

Regional associations develop for groups that have no autonomous professional organization. For example, professors and graduate students in the Midwest have an annual meeting at one of the universities in their region. The agenda is created jointly by the two groups, who hold separate and joint sessions. Seminars dominate the sessions; this indicates that inquiry is the dominant mode of learning at these conferences.

The gathering of professors has been replicated in New England at the annual conference of NASPA Region I. NASPA Region I also holds annual retreats for chief student affairs officers (CSAOs) from throughout New England. The CSAOs create agendas for these meetings. Retreat topics have ranged from the Meyers–Briggs Type Indicator to campus security, and the educational modes have ranged from instructional to inquiry. Informal networks of colleagues—CSAOs, graduate students, and professors—develop at these regional meetings. Campus visits, phone calls, and mailings between participants often follow the conferences.

Other types of gatherings may be concerned with specific topics rather than specific groups of people, for example, the condition of public or private higher education in a region. The Northeast region of the United States is noted for its institutions of private higher education. The Midwest is known for its public colleges and universities. Regional affiliations enable institutions to discuss their majority or minority needs within a geographic area. For example, the public colleges of New England contend with the Ivy League mystique, whether they are located in Connecticut, Rhode Island, or Maine. Because virtually all of the colleges in New England are located within 250 miles of each other, an association such as Region I of the NASPA can provide meaningful and accessible professional education activities for all their staffs.

The annual conference is the dominant educational activity of regional, as well as state and national, associations. Regions consolidate institutional and state resources so that prominent speakers and programs can be present at these conferences. In addition to an annual conference, many regions sponsor several one-day, drive-in workshops each year. Though the annual conference provides a range of activities for diverse professionals, the drive-in workshops promote specific learning for particular groups of practitioners, such as vandalism control techniques for residence hall directors.

During the early 1980s, the annual joint conference of NASPA and ACPA looked like a dinosaur—too big and too costly for the association and its members. This provoked the suggestion that the centralized national conference be replaced by mobile regional meetings. This suggestion might be realized in the future, when hotel and travel expenses increase. In the meantime, some national organizations have realized that their annual conferences improve when their planning committees represent the region in which the conference is to be held. Travel costs are reduced, regional attendance increases, the familiarity between committee members leads to better organization, and the strengths of the regional culture can be better shared with all of the association's members. Regional associations should provide the leadership for national conferences in the foreseeable future.

Limitations of Regional Associations. The limitations of regional associations stem from the size of multistate districts. Although most of the institutions in New England are located within 250 miles of each other, a similar range in a larger region omits most colleges and universities. Easy travel within most regions is prohibited, therefore, the effectiveness of the regional association is limited.

The large size of many regions means that budgets are dominated by travel and communication costs, rather than educational expenses. Travel expenses limit the allowable number of executive committee meetings in large regions. Although the members of executive committees pick up many expenses on their own, they cannot satisfy the general needs of a region by this means. Teleconferencing is less expensive, but it is not cheap. Regional associations often forego educational projects when their budgets are drained by travel. They cannot afford to implement activities on their own or seed them at the state or institutional levels.

Other situations also limit the effectiveness of regional associations. The semiannual meetings of some executive committees contain more introductions than business; more time is spent forming agendas than completing them. The use of state representatives on many executive committees protects the geography of the region but drains the budget and hampers the work of the committee. State representatives do not have easy access to each other to formulate and implement professional education projects. Cronyism develops when a few institutions or individuals control regional activities through their resources. When the input of new people and new ideas is limited, the professional education of regional association members is stifled.

National Associations

Professional associations can individually (or, more ideally, collectively) affect the success of professional education or individual campuses, in states, in regions, at the national level.

In a survey of the leadership of ACPA, Moore (1985) discovered that the top five purposes of the association were to (1) provide an annual convention for professional education of the members; (2) provide for and support ongoing professional education; (3) promote quality preparation for student affairs professionals; (4) encourage the development of a theoretical and conceptual base of the field; and (5) encourage the generation and dissemination of up-to-date knowledge about students.

Professional education seems to be the primary purpose of ACPA, NASPA, and most other professional associations. For example, NASPA's strategic plan (NASPA, 1984) lists the strengths of NASPA as a professional education agency for a wide range of student affairs practitioners.

In addition to their professional education purposes, the professional associations must identify current needs of the profession and its members. It must set standards and influence working conditions for the profession, both formally and informally. The professional association promulgates knowledge through its newsletters, journals, programs, workshops, and conferences. It promotes opportunities for professional development and enhances professional consciousness of student affairs among practitioners and among the general public.

These activities can stimulate the delivery of professional education on individual campuses, in states, and in regions. For example, the planning document of the American College Personnel Association stimulated the creation of the professional education center at the University of Vermont (see Chapter Five). A broader example is evident in the standards for master's degree education for student affairs professionals that have been adopted by the Council for the Advancement of Standards (CAS). That council is a consortium of twenty-one associations that serve student affairs practitioners. Their standards will influence master's degree programs on campuses across the nation.

Involvement in professional associations can help satisfy what Hall (1976) identifies as the task and socioemotional needs of people in various stages of professional development. (These resemble the professional development–stage needs described in Chapter Two.) Specifically, in the early-career stage, persons build skills and develop specialties. These professionals are moving toward autonomy but need the support of colleagues in the process. In the midcareer stage, the emphasis shifts from self-directed activity to outreach as professionals teach, coach, and share their skills with others. During this stage, people begin to examine their professional roles, both organizationally and beyond. Finally, in the late-career stage, professionals capitalize on the depth and breadth of their knowledge and practice. They act as consultants, often showcasing their talents outside the organization. Thus, Hall contends that professional associations can satisfy the needs of student affairs professionals at every stage of their careers.

It is widely agreed that professional associations should meet the stage needs of the student affairs practitioner, but they have not fulfilled all their obligations. In the professional and continuing education proposal of ACPA (Ender and others, 1984), the authors of the document suggest that professional associations need to be leaders in professional education, given the confusion about its processes, procedures, and priorities. Stamatakos (1981) contends that associations, rather than being the creative, courageous, assertive leaders that they need to be, have instead been timid reactors to many professional issues.

According to the model described in Chapter Two, professional associations provide inquiry learning, often meeting the additive needs of student affairs professionals. These characteristics can be muted or emphasized, according to the interests of the associations. For example, the Generativity Project of ACPA provides instructional media for student affairs professionals; NASPA maintains that NASPA is the primary association for chief student affairs officers.

National associations must be more than providers of professional education. They must also coordinate comprehensive professional education in student affairs. Their scope makes them the keepers of the model given in Chapter Two. They need to promote all the facets of that model for the whole gamut of practitioners in student affairs. A professionwide task force is a logical coordinating and promotion unit for professional education in student affairs.

National associations are bastions of the professional consciousness of student affairs (Stamatakos, 1981). That they are essential is unquestioned. That they can do more in regard to professional education seems equally unassailable. When they are good, they are very good. In a study of general higher education associations, Brown (1979) discovered strong support for them among presidents and chief academic officers. Comments such as the following were typical: "I derive much from these associations that I utilize to develop administrative concepts and techniques"; "One can learn more from others than from solemn contemplation."

According to the model in Chapter Two, professional associations should facilitate inquiry learning to meet the additive needs of student affairs professionals. Associations need to be involved in other modes of professional education as well. Through conferences, publications, and projects, national associations provide many resources of professional education. They need to ensure that other providers are also doing their part to provide institutional in-service, professional exchanges, statewide opportunities, developmental centers, and other professional education alternatives through a coordinated plan. (The latter, too, might be sketched from the model of professional education depicted in Chapter Two.)

Associations and the Professional Education Model

Statewide, regional, and national associations affect student affairs practitioners at all career levels. The interaction of formative, application, and additive professionals is encouraged by association membership. The dominant educational mode of associations is inquiry, which is delivered through formal seminars and informal gatherings of members. Associations also provide instruction for professionals about new theories and techniques in the field. The primary vehicle for delivering education is the annual conference. It can be augmented by drive-in workshops, retreats, or symposia at the regional and state levels.

Professional education alternatives must rejuvenate both counselors and administrators, but generally, associations for student affairs practitioners do not focus programs on the diverse staff-student assignments of their members. Some might charge that different associations serve professionals who have different types of interpersonal contact, but none of these organizations has deterred or encouraged membership on the basis of student-staff assignments.

Associations need to implement diverse professional education in student affairs through direct and indirect means. In terms of their own programs, most associations should provide more inquiry learning opportunities for their members, many of whom have additive professional needs. They might use the professional education model in Chapter Two to create programs that meet the needs of staff in different career stages. In addition, associations must go beyond their own activities to promote in-service programs, professional exchanges, and regional education centers for practitioners and graduate students. Leadership for these activities will be provided at the state and regional levels when it is encouraged at the national level. The authors suggest the formation of a national association task force that will encourage and coordinate the development of professional education activities for student affairs administrators and counselors. That task force must have the resources, charge, and continuity that will make its work successful.

References

Brown, D. *Leadership Vitality: A Workbook for Academic Administrators.* Washington, D.C.: American Council on Education, 1979.

Ender, K., Kane, N., Moore, L., Vasquez, M., and Miller, T. *Professional and Continuing Education Proposal.* Washington, D.C.: American College Personnel Association, 1984.

Hall, D. *Careers in Organizations.* Pacific Palisades, Calif.: Goodyear, 1976.

Healy, C. *Counseling Through the Life Stages.* Newton, Mass.: Allyn & Bacon, 1982.

Moore, L. *ACPA Goals Survey, 1985.* Report submitted to ACPA Executive Council, Bowling Green State University Library, Bowling Green, Ohio, 1985.

National Association of Student Personnel Administrators (NASPA). "NASPA Strategic Plan." Document approved by the NASPA Board of Directors. Louisville, Ky.: NASPA, 1984.

Schoonmaker, B. *College Student Personnel Association of New York, Evaluation and Planning Survey.* Albany: State University of New York, 1985.

Stamatakos, L. "Student Affairs Progress Towards Professionalism: Recommendations for Action." *Journal of College Student Personnel*, 1981, *22*, 197–206.

Marian Schrank is assistant vice-president for student affairs at the State University College at Brockport, New York.

Robert B. Young is associate professor and program adviser for higher education administration and coordinator of faculty development for the College of Education at Kent State University.

*The editors summarize the benefits of professional education
for individuals and institutions. Recommendations are
offered for a national effort to improve professional
education. Finally, readings are suggested for further
study about professional education in student affairs.*

Summary and Sources of Additional Information

Leila V. Moore, Robert B. Young

The chapters in this sourcebook have defined the status of professional education in student affairs, and they have offered suggestions about strengthening and diversifying professional education efforts for practitioners. The benefits of developing a more systematic and comprehensive approach to professional education are apparent in each chapter. Now, using a theoretical approach to professional education, let us propose and test generalizations about the fit between the needs of the individual and a professional education activity. Feeling prepared, competent, and up to date might influence the retention of professional student affairs staff. Certainly an awareness of changing needs for professional education permits the individual to take greater control over the design and selection of professional education activities. There are important roles for graduate faculty, both in continuing and in graduate education. Individual institutions can benefit by developing professional education activities that respond to the goals of the institution. Institutions also recognize the cost-effectiveness of retaining a competent and up-to-date staff.

The benefits enumerated here can be persuasive to the individual and to the institution in considering improvements in professional education. Such a grass-roots effort is necessary but may not be sufficient to influence the general upgrading of the entire field. As a profession, we

L. V. Moore, R. B. Young (eds.). *Expanding Opportunities for Professional Education.*
New Directions for Student Services, no. 37. San Francisco: Jossey-Bass, Spring 1987.

may not be recognizing the significance of the role of professional education in the professionalization of our field.

Toward a National Effort to Diversify Professional Education

For a model of professional education to benefit the profession as a whole, individual and institutional needs must be recognized and addressed by all who plan professional education activities, including state, regional, and national agencies. Likewise, as consumers of those activities, individuals and institutions need to know more about the professional activities they support. What target groups are programs addressing? The model presented in Chapter Two suggests that there are nine variable and a minimum of twenty-seven possible audiences for professional education activities. Instead of attempting to serve all professionals, perhaps national workshop and conference presenters could be encouraged to focus on a select few audiences. It would be up to convention planners to identify the audiences for specific programs and to ensure that all professional audiences are covered by the general array of programs.

New topics of concern to the profession need special attention by all professional associations. Perhaps a "new issues" section for conferences would focus on a topic in some depth by providing multiple opportunities for audiences to be taught the basic knowledge associated with that topic.

Presenters who have consistently distinguished themselves in one of the three modes of education (see the model) may be invited to fill in missing portions of the professional education activities of a scheduled conference. Such a pool of presenters could be developed through the examination of previous conference programs.

More demonstrations of the applications of theory to practice need to be made available—for example, new programs on the application of learning-style theory to a variety of settings, from counseling to faculty development.

We need to devote greater time and other resources to "exporting" professional education to individuals and institutions that cannot avail themselves of state, regional, or national resources. Audiocassette sales, teleconferencing, and videotaped learning programs (such as the workshop aspect of the Generativity Project of the American College Personnel Association) are examples of current efforts.

Finally, associations, sponsors of professional exchanges, and professional education centers need to form strong coalitions on behalf of professional education. Education is central to the establishment and maintenance of professions. The emergence of in-service requirements for professional credentialing underscores education's importance. As a profession, we need educational activities that meet professional criteria, have timely topics, possess quality of effort, pay systematic and equitable attention to all professionals, and are cost-effective (with respect also to travel, registration or tuition fees, and time). Individuals and institutions, the consumers of these expanded professional education activities, must insist on nothing less.

Readings About Professions and Professional Education

The literature about professions and professional education antedates most of the literature about professional education in student affairs. This chapter presents resources for student affairs practitioners who wish to study each of these subjects. Some of the resources are readily available; others are less so. The "classic" standing of some of these readings warrants their inclusion in this chapter, despite their age or their indirect relevance to the daily practices of student affairs work.

Argyris, C., and Schön, D. A. *Theory in Practice: Increasing Professional Effectiveness.* San Francisco: Jossey-Bass, 1974.
The authors examine the need for a theory concerning what shapes the actions practitioners take when confronted by new situations or problems in their professions. They contend that competence can only be developed when professionals understand the underlying theories that guide action or practice and how to use them.

Azzaretto, J. F. "Continuing Professional Educators as Change Agents." *The Journal of Continuing Higher Education,* 1986, *34* (1), 16–19.
A professional education specialist is a consultant to adults who are expanding and refining their professional competency. As consultants, these educators promote change in adult learners and assist them to adapt to those changes.

Beamer, E. G. "Continuing Education: A Professional Requirement." *Journal of Accountancy,* 1972, *133* (1), 33–39.
Continuing education is vital in professions. Substandard performance is usually the result of ignorance, not of willfulness. The professional is obligated to continue learning throughout the career. Formal education precedes certification; continuing education follows it. It has been suggested that knowledge will double every five years, if not more often.

Becker, H. S. "Some Problems of Professionalism." *Adult Education,* 1956, *6,* 101–105.
This article wrestles with the definition of *profession.* A professional establishes a client relationship and is bound by ethics to provide the best service possible. New professions have roots in other professions, a fact leading to divided loyalties.

72

Brodsky, N. "The Professional Education of Officers." *Phi Delta Kappan*, 1967, *48*, 429–432.
The military has long recognized the need for continuing education. It is necessary to broaden horizons and be prepared for increased responsibility. Education is supplemented by specialized training.

Chenault, J., and Burnford, F. *Human Services Professional Education.* New York: McGraw-Hill, 1978.
The purpose of professional education is to integrate human services literature across fields. It is stressed that classroom (theory) and practice-site (practical) training are not enough. Continuing education must stay abreast of new theories and methodologies. The author suggests a faculty-practitioner exchange program as well as an expansion of university learning to include skills and knowledge received in the "real world."

Clark, S. M., Corcoran, M., and Lewis, D. R. "The Case for an Institutional Perspective on Faculty Development." *The Journal of Higher Education*, 1986, *57* (2), 176–195.
The authors contend that there is a direct relationship between high faculty vitality (defined as high morale, high job satisfaction, and high professional productivity) and institutional vitality. They call for institutional support of faculty vitality through (1) administrative attitudes that recognize and reflect the concerns of faculty, (2) provisions of release time, (3) money and facilities for scholarly efforts, including efforts to improve teaching, and (4) assistance to faculty who are experiencing difficulties, such as inability to attract external funding for their research and need for further education in order to teach courses that meet new curriculum requirements. Many of the authors' recommendations for institutional response to faculty can be applied to student affairs staffs as well.

Dill, W. R., Crowston, W.B.S., and Elton, E. J. "Strategies for Self-Education." *Harvard Business Review*, 1965, *43*, 119–130.
The threat of professional obsolescence requires the pursuit of continuing education. Managers have to stay ahead of new graduates in their fields. Resources and incentives need to be provided, and formal training programs within organizations are recommended.

Dubin, S. S. "Obsolescence or Lifelong Education: A Choice for the Professional." *American Psychologist*, 1972, *27*, 486–498.
Past knowledge is continually being replaced or added to by new research and publications. Professionals are faced with the need to combat obsolescence. Suggested ways include continuing education, continuous training and retraining, science/education centers, and motivation with rewards.

Greenwood, E. "Attributes of a Profession." *Social Work,* 1957, *2*, 45–55.
The author states that the following characteristics are inherent in a profession: a particular body of knowledge, community sanction, authority, a code of ethics, and a formal and an informal culture. Success, especially for a new professional, depends on effective adjustment to the culture of the profession.

Houle, C. O. *Continuing Learning in the Professions.* San Francisco: Jossey-Bass, 1980.
Houle describes the evolution of professions. He advocates the concept of dynamic professionalization, instead of professional status, for occupational fields. He relates this concept to three modes of continuous learning: instruction, inquiry, and performance.

The Journal of Continuing Higher Education.
Published by the Association for Continuing Higher Education, this journal may be new to many student affairs professionals. Following is a quotation from *The Journal*'s guidelines for preparation of manuscripts: *"The Journal* welcomes manuscripts on organization and administration of continuing higher education; new programs in continuing higher education—degree, certificate, credit, credit free, and community service; student services in continuing higher education; research in the various fields of continuing higher education." *The Journal of Continuing Higher Education* is circulated in January, April, July, and September.

Long, L. D. "The Evaluation of Continuing Education Efforts." *American Journal of Public Health and the Nation's Health,* 1969, *59*, 967–973.
Continuing education improves competencies and enables professionals to deal with the impact of new knowledge. New technologies and information prevent completion of learning about a field from taking place solely within formal educational training.

Parrett, J. L. "Continuing Professional Education: The Blurred Image." *Journal of Continuing Higher Education,* 1986, *34* (3), 9–12.
The author stresses the importance of differentiating between continuing *higher* education and continuing *professional* education. She asserts that the instructional methods employed by these two forms of education are quite different. Lifelong learning for personal development guides the selection of instructional approaches for continuing higher education. However, continuing professional education is designed to fill gaps in professional preparation and to refine or maintain current skills. Instructional methods for continuing professional education must be more specific to the skill, include ongoing assessment of skill development, and rely heavily on practice.

Shimberg, B. S. "Continuing Education and Licensing." In D. W. Vermilye (ed.), *Relating Work and Education: Current Issues in Higher Education 1977*. San Francisco: Jossey-Bass, 1977.
The author discusses the proliferation of new knowledge and the need for professionals to keep pace. He is concerned that voluntary continuing education is not sufficient and identifies problems of continuing education that need to be addressed.

Sneed, J. T. "Continuing Education in the Professions." *Journal of Higher Education*, 1972, *43*, 223–238.
The author expresses the main purpose of continuing education and goes into a detailed discussion of costs and benefits, government subsidies for continuing education, and other sources of funding. The author explores the contributions and responsibilities of higher education to continuing education.

Stark, J. S., Lowther, M. A., Hagerty, B.M.K., and Orczyk, C. "A Conceptual Framework for the Study of Preservice Professional Programs in Colleges and Universities." *The Journal of Higher Education*, 1986, *57* (3), 231–258.
In this article, the authors explain and discuss a systematic way for examining graduate education programs. The basic elements of their approach include examination of methods of education; the environment in which the education occurs; influences from external sources, such as government policies and funding, licensing, and placement of graduates; influences from other programs in the institution; and influences from the program itself, such as composition and expertise of faculty, purpose of the program, and time required to complete degree, curriculum, and continuing professional education. For those interested in professional education, the value of this approach is its identification of several ways in which professional education relates to and influences the shape of graduate education programs.

Stern, M. (ed.). *Power and Conflict in Continuing Professional Education*. Belmont, Calif.: Wadsworth, 1983.
This book addresses questions about who should develop and offer continuing professional education. It includes a discussion of professional relicensure as it relates to professional education and poses the dilemma of voluntary versus required continued professional education.

Toombs, W. E., and Lindsay, C. A. "Continuing Education for Professionals: A Practice-Oriented Approach." *Journal of Continuing Higher Education*, 1985, *33* (1), 8–13.

This article contains a description of The Continuing Professional Education Project at The Pennsylvania State University. The project began in 1980. Its objectives were to bring selected professions and a selected university into greater cooperation for professional education; to present programs that represented the needs of the practitioners as closely as possible; and to create permanent links between selected professional associations and The Pennsylvania State University on behalf of continuing professional education.

Young, K. E. "Graduate Education and Continuing Education." In M. J. Pelczar, Jr., and L. C. Solomon (eds.), *Keeping Graduate Programs Responsive to National Needs*. New Directions for Higher Education, no. 46. San Francisco: Jossey-Bass, 1984.
This article explores the rapidly growing need for noncredit learning, particularly in continuing professional education. Young stresses that graduate education will need to focus on education for practitioners.

Student Affairs Resources

Bentley, J. C. "Developing Effective Teams: Why and How?" In C. H. Foxley (ed.), *Applying Management Techniques*. New Directions for Student Services, no. 9. San Francisco: Jossey-Bass, 1980.
The complexity of organizations and the differentiation of work have made it vital that professionals collaborate. This need poses a problem, however, and particularly for men, who value their self-reliance and independence. The author suggests that the greatest administrative challenge is narrowing the gap between a person's individual goals and the goals of the organization. He examines and compares mechanistic and organic groups and describes five stages for team-building intervention.

Canon, H. "Toward Professionalism in Student Affairs: Another Point of View." *Journal of College Student Personnel*, 1982, *23*, 468–473.
The author addresses the problems created by lack of standards in student affairs programs. Excellent and marginal programs coexist. The most important goal of the curriculum is to impart a comprehensive understanding of the environment of higher education institutions. The author stresses the importance of applying developmental literature to programming in student affairs.

Canon, H. "Developmental Tasks for the Profession: The Next 25 Years." *Journal of College Student Personnel*, 1984, *25* (2), 105–111.
Canon addresses the developmental tasks for the future of student personnel professionals. He asks what will replace the *in loco parentis* principle on campuses. Mutual responsibility between students and administrators,

according to developmental theory, should provide the opportunity both for student growth and for minimized institutional risk. Finally, Canon stresses the importance of support and caring among colleagues on each college campus.

Carpenter, D. S., and Miller, T. K. "An Analysis of Professional Development in Student Affairs Work." *National Association of Student Personnel Administrators Journal,* 1981, *19,* 2-11.
Borrowing from psychological theory, the authors describe various stages of development among student affairs administrators. Their article reports the use of the Student Affairs Professional Development Inventory to assess the developmental stages of administrators.

Garland, P. H. *Serving More Than Students: A Critical Need for College Student Personnel Services.* ASHE–ERIC Higher Education Report No. 7. Washington, D.C.: Association for the Study of Higher Education, 1985.
Garland, focuses on the role of student affairs staff members as "integrators" of the contributions made by students, staff, and faculty to the educational environment of the institution. In this role, the student affairs integrator contributes to the campus community by effectively and efficiently managing time, money, and people; leading institutional response to changes in higher education; specializing in organizational development; planning; assessing the campus environment; and explaining to faculty, staff, and students how theories of student development are applied to enrich the campus environment.

Nygreen, G. T. "Professional Status for Student Personnel Administrators." *NASPA Journal,* 1968, *5,* 283-291.
Although student personnel administrators are useful, they are not necessary. Their functions can be performed by faculty members. The implication is that faculty are professionals and student personnel administrators are only bureaucrats. Unable to operate autonomously, student personnel administrators are caught up in the conflicts of professionalism (since they are oriented toward goals and standards), administration (since they are responsible for policy implementation), and service to others.

Owens, H., Meabon, D., Suddick, D., and Klein, A. "Implementation of Management Techniques: Myth or Reality?" *NASPA Journal,* 1981, *18* (4), 14-21.
Throughout higher education, the continued expectation of accountability has resulted in the suggestion to adapt business management principles to the higher education area. The article provides a comparison of various management techniques implemented in three major administrative areas in colleges and universities: academic affairs, business affairs, and student affairs. The appropriateness of these concepts is considered.

Penn, J. R. "Professional Accreditation: A Key to Excellence." *Journal of College Student Personnel,* 1974, *15,* 257–259.
The author restates the need to define accreditation standards for student personnel workers and predicts that otherwise the field of student personnel work may vanish. His major concern is for quality of the graduate curricula and programs being offered in the field. He recommends establishing a national accreditation board for the field.

Sandeen, A. "Student Services in the '80s: A Decade of Decisions." *NASPA Journal,* 1982, *19* (3), 2–9.
Sandeen expresses the need to expand student affairs activities beyond past roles. The success and growth of the field depend on its flexibility and willingness to move into new areas of responsibility. It must identify new needs and find ways to meet them. Staff cannot assume passive roles.

Shaffer, R. H. "Critical Dimensions of Student Affairs in the Decades Ahead." *Journal of College Student Personnel,* 1984, *25,* 112–114.
Shaffer identifies new campus trends and subsequent forces that are reshaping the student affairs field. Failure to identify and respond to these changes will devalue the contribution of student affairs on campus. Administrators must become leaders who anticipate and prevent problems and who are flexible and adaptable. In part, this requires continuing education.

Sims, J. M., and Foxley, C. H. "Job Analysis, Job Descriptions, and Performance Appraisal Systems." In C. H. Foxley (ed.), *Applying Management Techniques.* New Directions for Student Services, no. 9. San Francisco: Jossey-Bass, 1980.
The authors recommend that student services administrators institute clearly defined personnel systems for their particular areas of responsibility. These systems provide a tool for effective management as well as a developmental approach to working with staff. The authors include an in-depth investigation of three management techniques: job analyses, job descriptions, and performance appraisal.

Stamatakos, L. C. "Student Affairs Progress Toward Professionalism: Recommendations for Action." *Journal of College Student Personnel,* 1981, *22,* 105–113 and 197–206.
The author reviews and addresses eight criteria, presented by Wrenn and Darley in 1949, concerning student affairs as a profession. He stresses the importance of determining the appropriate place for student affairs in higher education. Emphasis is given to developing standards for accreditation, and comment is made on the lack of reasonable admission standards and on the absence of standards for preparation. The need for existing faculty to update their knowledge and skills in the profession is explored.

Wood, L., Winston, R. B., Jr., and Polkosnik, M. C. "Career Orientations and Professional Development of Young Student Affairs Professionals." *Journal of College Student Personnel*, 1985, *26*, 532–539.
This article reviews a professional development model in student affairs (see Carpenter and Miller, 1981, cited previously). It explores career anchors, the need for mobility, and the correlation between career orientations and four professional developmental stages. It is suggested that people leave student affairs because they desire greater autonomy.

Leila V. Moore is currently director of Career Path Associates and assistant director for student organizations and program development at the Pennsylvania State University. She was formerly a professor of counseling and student personnel at the State University of New York at Albany, at the Pennsylvania State University, and at Bowling Green State University.

Robert B. Young is associate professor and program adviser for higher education administration and coordinator of faculty development for the College of Education at Kent State University.

APPENDIX
Interview Protocol for Assessing Professional Education
Needs of Student Affairs Staff

Instructions to Interviewer: The interview questions below are arranged from the specific to the general. Their sequence helps you and the interviewee to develop rapport before you engage in the evaluation activity at the end of the interview. Please allow approximately thirty minutes for this interview.

1. How many years has it been since you started working full-time? Include years of full-time employment both in and out of student affairs. [*Interviewer:* This question confirms placement on the professional development dimension of the model.]

2. What degrees do you now hold? When did you earn them? [*Interviewer:* This is used to identify the mode of education and to determine a plan for the doctorate when the interviewee does not have one.]

3. How many years have you been in your current job? If you supervise staff, how many (full- and part-time, professional, and other)? What is the average percent of time you spend weekly with students? With staff or faculty (both in your own office and elsewhere on campus)? Do you have a mentor now? If not, do you want one? [*Interviewer:* These questions identify both professional development level and interpersonal involvement level.]

4. Are you enrolled in any graduate classes now? If so, do you enjoy them? [*Interviewer:* Expand here if interviewee responds "yes and no" by asking person to tell you what is enjoyable and what is not.] Do you like to learn by enrolling in graduate classes? [*Interviewer:* This question helps to identify the mode of education.]

5. What are your career plans for the next three years? Do you expect to change jobs? If so, what would you anticipate as the change? [*Interviewer:* Interviewee may have in mind not a job title but rather the types of work responsibilities she or he would prefer.] What do you think you need to do to qualify for this anticipated job change? [*Interviewer:* The first part of the question identifies any change in ratio of staff-student contact. The second part gives you information about the content areas that might motivate the interviewee to seek professional education.]

6. What was the last national convention you attended? What was the main benefit, personal or professional, that you derived from attending? [*Interviewer:* Here, you gain some knowledge of the interviewee's preferred type of education.]

7. What was the last regional workshop or meeting you attended? What was the main benefit, personal or professional, that you derived from attending?

8. What was the last professional education activity you partici-

pated in? What was the main benefit, personal or professional, that you derived from attending? [*Interviewer:* Question 7 has the same purpose as Question 6. Question 8 adds to your information about the interviewee's preferred mode of education, and it provides additional information about the individual's level of professional development.]

9. Have you had a mentor? Are you a mentor? If not, would you like to be one? With what kind of person would you feel most comfortable establishing a mentor relationship? [*Interviewer:* Some individuals might describe themselves as mentors to students, but not to staff. Since the professional development dimension involves staff mentoring, you may be able to suggest these mentoring activities.]

10. *Interviewer:* Have the interviewee identify his or her present position on each of the dimensions of the professional education model. Indicate that you will be doing the same thing, using the information gathered in the interview. When you and the interviewee have completed this activity, review your perceptions and discuss any differences. Attempt to come to agreement when differences in perception emerge.

Index